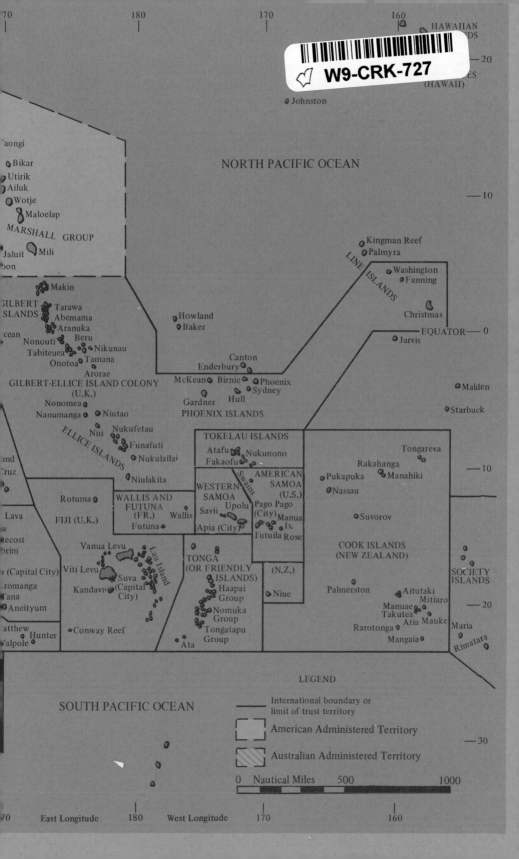

National Security
and
International ...
in the Pacific

National Security
and
International Trusteeship
in the Pacific

To my former students in the Africa
and Pacific courses at the
Naval War College

ACKNOWLEDGEMENTS

I would above all like to give my hearty thanks to Captain John L. Butts, USN, who in many ways helped to complete this volume. My thanks also go to Captain H. B. Robertson, USN; Captain E. J. Wielki, USN; Captain H. S. Parrish, USN; Captain W. H. Borchert, USN; Colonel Clinton E. Granger, Jr., USA; Professor J. Kenneth McDonald; Mr. Glen B. Ruh; Mrs. Rosemary Epting; and Mrs. Barbara Bowen.

Preface

At the end of World War II, the United States eagerly anticipated a withdrawal from overseas responsibilities and a return to concentration on internal affairs. This euphoria proved shortlived, as it soon became apparent that this country was the only power able to assist other nations, economically broken and politically weak in the aftermath of war, toward peacetime recovery and military security. The Truman Doctrine and the Marshall Plan were American responses to various post-war challenges.

One challenge, not much publicized, was administering the non self-governing islands of the Western Pacific, previously occupied by the Japanese. The history of U.S. "trusteeship" of these many islands over a period of more than two decades is replete with controversy. Domestically, a central issue has been the Department of the Navy's cognizance versus the Department of the Interior's cognizance. Internationally, the debate has centered in the United Nations, with Russia the most active proponent of immediate self-government for all of these territories, regardless of size, population, or self-governing ability.

Of course, inherent in the history of these islands is their relation to the long-term security interests of the United States. As our military base structure in the Western Pacific is reduced, these trust territories assume greater significance. As the Soviet naval, fishing, merchant, and oceanographic fleets progressively expand their operations across the Pacific Ocean, Russian political efforts in the United Nations to remove these islands from U.S. control can be expected to increase.

This book is most timely. It is the product of four years of scholarly seminars held at the U.S. Naval War College. It addresses the contrast between trusteeship and security aspects of the territories. In dealing with these themes, the officers who have contributed have provided, I believe, a valuable historical commentary, a perceptive analysis of present problems, and a considered judgment of possible future options open to the United States.

R. G. COLBERT
Vice Admiral, U.S. Navy
Former President, U.S. Naval War College

Contents

Introduction

This symposium contains representative essays prepared by officers of the United States Naval War College on a specific and controversial theme: national security and international trusteeship in the Pacific. The basic issue can be stated briefly and clearly: the United States fought the war in the Pacific to defeat Japan, and, as a subordinate war aim, to gain control of the Marshall, Caroline and Mariana islands; yet, at the end of the war, the United States agreed to place these islands under the supervision of the United Nations. Thus the dilemma of international supervision and self-determination, on the one hand, and of national security on the other.

Admiral Colbert well describes the present significance of these island groups in the foreword. The essays that follow explain the problem in historical perspective and deal with the dilemma of international supervision and self-determination under the auspices of the United States, Australia, and New Zealand. The essays raise several major questions. What is the strategic significance of the islands? What is their future and how is it to be determined? What role will the United Nations play? And, perhaps most important of all, how has American influence and rule changed, for better or worse, the lives of Micronesians?

A word needs to be said about the creation of the trusteeship system in order to understand the present situation. In 1919 the great powers established the mandates system, by which under Article 22 of the Covenant of the League of Nations peoples of the former German and Turkish empires were to be held as a "sacred trust of civilization." Historians argue about the extent to which this was a revolutionary concept, but most have traditionally stated that its immediate origins was a combination of Wilsonian idealism and the hard-headed realism of Prime Minister William M. Hughes of Australia. The clash between those two famous personalities—which amounted to a personal feud—nearly ruptured the peace negotiations following World War I. In fact the "idealism" of Wilson and the "realism" of Hughes did not contradict each other: the President not only wanted to root out "imperialism" as a cause of war in the Pacific, but also to establish a system of international control that would check possible Japanese aggression; the Prime Minister aimed for measures to defend Australasia, and acquiesced in the rhetoric of international idealism when he received assurance that the mandates system would not interfere with the fiscal and immigration policies of Australia. In short, the President wanted to protect the United States against possible Japanese expansion while the Prime Ministers of Australia and New Zealand sought to protect their countries by the creation or preservation of an "island shield"— the same concept employed today in regard to Micronesia.

It is perhaps ironic that the United States, by holding Micronesia as a "strategic trusteeship," possesses rights that far exceed those that Japan held under the Class C mandate. It could indeed be argued that the unique classification of "strategic trusteeship" means little more than sovereignty in all but name. The United States possesses the right to fortify the islands and to take virtually all other measures deemed necessary for purposes of defense. Yet during World War II the United States explicitly accepted the principles of trusteeship as embodied in the Charter of the United Nations. Various authors—including prominent members of the Truman administration—have described the subsequent decision to place the Pacific Islands under international control as one of the most controversial of the immediate post-war era. A definitive analysis of the argumentation that led to the United States's obtaining a "strategic trust" remains to be written, and cannot be written until the complete opening of governmental archives. In the meantime, the point to be made is simply that the United States decided in favor of trusteeship. This meant supervision by the Trusteeship Council of the United Nations.

The Charter of the United Nations describes the basic object of the trusteeship system. Essentially, the Charter authorizes the Trusteeship Council to: (a) consider reports submitted by the administering authority; (b) accept petitions; (c) provide for periodical visits of inspection on behalf of the United Nations. Despite various disagreements, relations between the Trusteeship Council and the United States have gone relatively smoothly. The basic disagreement between the United Nations and the United States in this regard arose when the President of the General Assembly in early 1962 appointed a special committee to inquire into the problem of final and unconditional liquidation of colonialism. The following nations were represented: Australia, Cambodia, Ethiopia, India, Italy, Madagascar, Mali, Poland, Syria, Tanganyika, Tunisia, the U.S.S.R., the United Kingdom, the United States, Uruguay, Venezuela, and Yugoslavia. Subsequently the General Assembly added Bulgaria, Chile, Denmark, Iran, Iraq, Ivory Coast, and Sierra Leone, thus making the committee popularly known as the "Committee of the 24." Conspicuously missing from the Committee were France and Portugal, who both continue to hold dependent territories. The Committee's investigation in the Pacific ranged from Pitcairn (land area about 2 square miles, population about 100) to New Guinea (land area about 180,000, population in excess of 2 million). The land area of Micronesia is about 680 square miles with a population of approximately 90,000. From those statistics one can quickly gather that New Guinea, some of whose inhabitants still do not possess knowledge of the use of the wheel, will pose to Australia most enormous difficulties in decolonization. In some ways the problem of the United States and her island dependencies will be equally difficult—or, according to most of the members of the Committee of the 24, quite simple, if the United States immediately were to give the islanders independence. To make a long story short, the Committee so persistently and shrilly denounced British administration in islands such as St. Helena and Tristan da Cunha, and so vituperously demanded independence for Micronesia that the United Kingdom and the United States have withdrawn from the Committee.

Whatever ideological or any other position one might take in regard to the actions of the Committee of the 24, it is clear that they have raised basic issues. They are true in saying that the United States permitted the neglect of the islands during the Navy's administration of the islands until 1951, when the Department of the Interior accepted responsibility for them. Naval authorities allowed the deterioration of the "infra-structure" built by the Japanese, and health conditions grew so bad that as late as 1966 the World Health Organization deplored the lack of sufficient sanitary and medical facilities. But it is a matter of historical fact that improvement has been made in those areas, in part because of Peace Corps workers. Although political authority is vested in a high commissioner appointed by the President, since 1965 there has been an elected bicameral legislature, commonly known as the Congress of Micronesia. This body has pursued the most basic issue raised by the Committee of the 24, that of self-determination, to which the United States is committed. In recent years, at least, the United States has been fully aware of that commitment. In 1967 President Johnson proposed a plebiscite to be held no later than 1972, a plebiscite not about independence but about the future government and political relationship of the island groups. In mid-1969 Secretary of the Interior Hickel visited Micronesia, hoping to work out plans for the plebiscite and promising steps toward self-government. In response, he got proposals ranging from amalgamation of the entire area with Guam, to "free association," to "unincorporated territories," to "commonwealth status," to unilateral independence, Rhodesian style. At meetings held in 1970 these various proposals were debated extensively between Mr. Hickel and a Micronesian delegation. The specific issue boiled down to defining "Commonwealth Status in Free Association with the United States." The controversy became complex, involving local participation administration, equal wages to Micronesians and Americans, development of roads and electrical plants, and duty-free imports of Micronesian produces. One dominant theme of the negotiations that needs to be pointed out is the Micronesian belief that the United States intends to seize more land for military installations. According to official reports, at present there are no military bases in Micronesia (though of course Bikini and Eniwetok in the Marshalls have been used as nuclear-test sites). In any case the discussions resulted in stalemate. All that can be said is that the chances of a plebiscite in the near future are remote.

Where does this leave us in regard to self-determination? To put it pessimistically in the words of one of the principle authorities, Professor Rupert Emerson of Harvard, "All people do *not* have the right of self-determination: they have never had it, and they never will have it. The changing content of natural law in the era of de-colonization has brought no change in this basic proposition." Regardless whether Professor Emerson's dictum is right or wrong in regard to Micronesia, it can be said with certainty that, though Micronesia is a dependency of the United States, Micronesia is economically dependent on the United States. To quote another expert on the subject, Captain Dwight A. Lane (USN), currently U. S. Naval Attaché in New Zealand, "until the Micronesians feel that their economic and social future is guaranteed, and until the United States is assured that national security will not be jeopardized, there can be no final solution."

One popular assumption about why there is as yet no "final solution" is that the Soviet Union is attempting to undermine the position of the United States in the Pacific. I would like to pose the proposition differently, or at least try to get to the heart of the strategic debate. To begin, there have been changes in the strategic position of the United States throughout the world in very recent years—changes brought about by technological advances in weapons and weapons systems, the increased military capabilities of the Soviet Union, near revolution in the western economic community, and domestic unrest in the United States combined with a revival of isolationist sentiment (in the words of Representative Wilbur D. Mills, "At present we seem to be getting right back to where we were after World War I"). Despite these changes the islands of the Pacific still give the United States an advantage—some would call it a "denial" advantage—not held by any other major power. In the near future there is no apparent political or military shift which is likely to lessen the strategic value of American control of the islands west of Hawaii. Even over the longer term, whatever the degree of accommodation achieved with China and whatever the outcome of negotiations with the Soviet Union regarding limitation of strategic arms and reduction of forces, the United States still will continue to have strategic advantages because of its position in the Pacific. Indeed, that position might well be enhanced by the attainment of a strategic "status quo" acceptable to the governments of the United States, the Soviet Union, China, and, not least, Japan. Attainment of such a position must be regarded, even optimistically, as a long-range project. Negotiations with the Soviet Union on strategic arms limitations are in progress, but, so far, according to published reports, the results are still ponderable. China? Who knows? What is the yardstick by which to measure recent American initiatives? And what is the future of Russian-Chinese relations? Since the United States presumably wants better relations with both countries, the point hinges on whether either the Soviets or the Chinese—particularly the latter—retreat again to the position of the "friend of my enemy is my enemy."

The point to be taken from this analysis is that decisions of the United States as to the future of the strategic trust territories are most likely to be made, in the foreseeable future at least, without the benefit of resolution of some of the more pressing problems involving the Soviet Union and China. But even if some of the more vexing questions of American-

Russian-Chinese relations can be partially resolved, there would still be the issue of Japan's future role, a role which probably will be decided more by the nature of possible future accord between the United States and China and related external factors then by deliberate, internal design by Japan. This interpretation is necessarily speculative, but it can be said with certainty that Japan's choice of directions or re-orientation in international relations will be a driving consideration of all deliberations involving the position of the United States in the Pacific. To put the proposition in its bluntest form, one school of thought holds that, if the United States were to withdraw from Micronesia, Japan might try to re-occupy its former mandates, not only for strategic but also for economic reasons. This speculation has ramifications that affect other nations in the Pacific basin as well: if the Japanese are on the line between California and Manila, they also are on the line between Tokyo and Sydney.

As for Russian designs, it is entirely true that representatives of the Soviet Union have persistently denounced American "imperialism" in the Pacific. Whether for political or strategic considerations (and the latter appears the more likely), the Soviet aim is the recreation in the Pacific of small, fragmented polities—islands or island groups which would no longer be under the control or sway of the United States or any other western power. Now, it can be argued—and one eminent historian of the Pacific, Professor C. Hartley Grattan puts the case forcefully—that these strategic considerations are insignificant because Micronesia, in his words, has "*no* strategic significance to anyone, except possibly as a United States 'storage' place or testing ground." On the other hand, it can be argued that, technological advances and advanced weapons systems notwithstanding, American officials still see specific strategic advantages to a continued American presence in the strategic trust territories. As Geoffrey Hudson, the former director of the Far Eastern Center at Oxford, has written, "It is certainly difficult to believe that Micronesia has *no* strategic significance. . . . Surely in the event of a naval war or confrontation, it would make a difference if one side or the other had weapons deployed on some of the islands." To put it differently, if United States naval authorities are agreed that Micronesia has no strategic significance, there surely is no problem; it would be best to give independence to the islands as soon as possible, as there would be no reason to disagree with the Committee of the 24 (though the Micronesians themselves would probably take a different view, if only for economic reasons). But if the islands *are* considered to have strategic value, the United States appears to be in a strong position for keeping effective control over them. It is natural that the Soviet Union in building up its new naval power in all the oceans (and in the Pacific the Soviet fishing, merchant, and oceanographic fleets have progressively expanded) should seek to reduce the American position in the Pacific by the recreation of the island groupings before the "take-over" by the western powers. But whatever the Soviet Union can achieve in the United Nations—and whatever the influence of the Committee of the 24—the status of the islands cannot legally be altered except by a decision of the Security Council, which would be subject to American veto.

To put the argument in its most extreme form, the greatest danger to the American position in the Pacific would arise from local politics (which some American officials believe might be influenced by the Soviets) in an independent Micronesia where a party might get power on a demand for neutrality and removal of American facilities—or possible facilities. If, therefore, the United States wishes to prevent this happening, it will be essential to retain reserve powers restricting the right of local authorities to take any measures which would be incompatible with the possible exercise of United States strategic rights.

So runs the "hard line" argument, which, though to some may appear alarmist and unrealistic, appears to reflect a certain trend in American official thought. Micronesia remains the "island shield" of the United States in the Pacific.

In the chapters that follow, Captain Miller begins the discussion of present day problems in the Pacific by examining the broad aspects of the future of all the islands and asking what role the United Nations is having and will have in shaping the destinies of the peoples of the Pacific. Following Commander Wilson's general account of the trusteeship territories south of the equator, Colonel Dodenhoff and Commander Munsey provide an interesting commentary that touches on the exploration of the island groups; they also compare American and New Zealand rule, and, among other things, raise the important question of the future of overseas dependencies of the United States such as American Samoa. Captain Butts, in the chapter on New Guinea, concludes that the question of independence for a country so far removed from today's technology will be one of the most excruciating experiences in the process of decolonization.

Shifting north of the Equator, Captain Lane examines in detail the issue of self-determination in Micronesia. Colonel Haigwood re-explores the myth that the Japanese systematically fortified the mandated islands. In the next chapter Colonel Adams extensively reviews the question of annexation versus trusteeship at the end of World War II, and points out that one of the Truman administration's most bitter internal controversies was whether or not to place the islands under the supervision of the United Nations. He raises strategic, political, and economic questions that are discussed specifically in regard to the Carolines, Marianas, and Marshalls in the following three chapters. Commander Nystrom deals with the political problems of the Carolines, while in the chapter on the Marianas Commander Lincoln devotes special attention to problems of economic development. Colonel Hunter, in the chapter on the Marshalls, raises the most interesting question of American impact on indigenous societies and the process of social change. The concluding chapter by Captains Miller and Thompson draw together the main themes of the symposium by emphasizing the dilemma of the world community attempting to promote the principle of self-determination in areas where chances of independent viability are remote.

The views expressed in the symposium are based entirely on unclassified, open sources and reflect the personal ideas of the authors and not necessarily those of the Department of Defense or any other governmental agency.

As in any symposium dealing with problems of the present, there is bound to be disagreement among the authors, some echoing tones of the cold war of the 1950s, others looking forward to accommodation with both Russia and China. The symposium was designed to encourage a frank exchange of ideas, not to reach a consensus. To me one of the main points is not only that these military officers have a grasp of the political and strategic problems of the Pacific, but that they are also fully aware of the economic, sociological, and even ecological aspects of Micronesia. In other words, these essays demonstrate that the Pacific islands should indeed be a *TRUST* and not merely points of strategic value.

National Security
and
International Trusteeship
in the Pacific

1 / The United Nations and Oceania

William O. Miller,

*Captain, Judge Advocate General's Corps,
United States Navy*

Stretching from the west coasts of the Americas to the Asian mainland is the earth's most formidable water barrier—the Pacific Ocean. This mammoth body of water comprises two-thirds of the ocean area of the world and a full one-third of the earth's surface. Interspersed throughout this vast area are literally thousands of islands, divided generally into the island chains of Melanesia, Micronesia, and Polynesia. Since western man has navigated these waters, these islands of Oceania have been sought after jealously by the world's powers—first for the pleasure and sojourn they offered, then for their wealth, and finally for their strategic value. The peoples of these islands were extremely diverse in racial background, culture and social customs, and they had only one thing in common. They were organized, if at all, into small, fragmented, premodern societies, with no effective capacity to resist domination by any power interested in exercising it.[1]

The resulting scramble for hegemony culminated in the late 1800's in large island groupings gradually becoming subject to the colonial administration of one or another of the western powers. Since that time, as national powers have ebbed and flowed, sovereignty or control over most of these islands has undergone frequent change. This is particularly true of the islands of Micronesia which have been under the successive control of Spain, Germany, Japan, and now the United States. These Pacific outposts became, in the early days of World War II, "footsteps" for a mili-

A version of this chapter has appeared in the *Naval War College Review*, XXI, 10 June 1969.

taristic Japanese expansion southward toward Australia, and they formed "a series of great spider webs 'made to order' " as one Japanese admiral said, "to catch any unwary flies that tried to cross the Pacific."[2] Later they served the same purpose for the United States and its Allies in their successful efforts to choke off the exposed extensions of Japanese military power, and they provided successive rungs in the U.S. ladder constructed for assault on imperial Japan.

The strategic significance of Oceania is a fact of modern history which underscores Admiral Mahan's classic analysis of the dependence of effectively exercised seapower on strategically located land bases.[3] Located as they are athwart the maritime lines of communication from the Western Hemisphere to Southeast Asia, these islands once provided operating bases from which the sea lanes supporting the projection of power into this area were severed—and they could do so again.

The United Nations has a special bearing on the situation in the Pacific because of its "Committee on the Situation with regard to the Implementation of the Declaration on the Granting of Independence to Colonial Countries and Peoples," commonly known as the "Special Committee of Twenty-four." This chapter will trace the historical antecedents of the Special Committee of Twenty-four, thereby putting the present-day problems of the Pacific into perspective.

From the timid beginnings of Article 22 of the Covenant of the League of Nations, the efforts of the international community to bring about a universal application of the principle of self-determination of peoples have assumed an ever-expanding scope. In the aftermath of World War I the problem of the disposition of former enemy colonial possessions was resolved by the creation of the League of Nations mandate system under which these territories were theoretically taken under international control. Such territories whose peoples were ". . . not yet able to stand by themselves under the strenuous conditions of the modern world" were entrusted to the tutelage of "more advanced nations" who were willing to accept the "sacred trust of civilization" and to provide for their "well-being and development."

Whatever defects may have existed in this system, and there were many,[4] it must be said that the very creation of a scheme of even tenuous international control over colonial areas represented a dramatic departure from prior practices. It assumes even greater significance when it is recognized that this was a voluntary act on the part of the western nations whose past policies had been to extend their own individual imperial control over widely dispersed colonial possessions.[5] While it may be true that the international control of the League was of the colonial powers' own design, it did signal the beginnings of a reform movement under which the entire international community would seek to oversee the transformation of dependent peoples into self-determination.

The Second World War gave additional impetus to international concern about the problems of dependent peoples. Particularly was this true in the United States where almost all responsible officials, including the President, were of the view that the days of colonialism were past and that in the new, postwar order there should be a comprehensive trusteeship system embracing all dependent people.[6] Although no such all-pervasive system developed, there were significant advances made toward more effective international supervision.

This new order for dependent peoples was to be structured on two basic concepts: first, an expanded and improved international trusteeship system with a view toward the ultimate "self-government or independence" of the trust territories,[7] and second, a declaration by the colonial powers of their duties toward, and the rights of, the dependent peoples of all territories who "have not yet attained a full measure of self-government."[8]

The newly created trusteeship system functioned under an institutionalized Trusteeship Council composed equally of administering and non-administering powers.[9] To be placed under this system were the territories formerly held under League mandate, those liberated from enemy control as a result of World War II, and those territories which might be voluntarily placed under the system by any of the colonial powers.[10] Only ten of the formerly mandated territories plus Somaliland were placed under Trusteeship Council supervision.[11] In the Pacific area these included the Trust Territory of the Pacific Islands, formerly mandated to Japan but now under the administration of the United States; the Trust Territory of New Guinea under Australian administration; and Western Samoa and Nauru under New Zealand and Australian administration, respectively.

The basic objectives of the trusteeship system are those of Article 1 of the United Nations Charter and all territories held under League of Nations mandate at the time of adoption of the articles concerning trust territories were designated as participants under the revised system of administration. The Trusteeship Council was authorized by the Charter to:

a. Consider reports submitted by the Administering Authority.

b. Accept petitions and examine them in consultation with the Administering Authority.

c. Provide for periodic visits to the respective trust territories at times agreed upon with the Administering Authority.

d. Take these and other actions in conformity with the terms of the Trusteeship agreements.

Specific trusteeship agreements were entered into with the administering powers stating specifically the terms under which the trust was to be exercised. The Trusteeship Council was invested with significant powers to oversee the exercise of these trust agreements. It was given authority to consider reports to be submitted regularly by the administering powers, to receive and examine petitions from inhabitants of the territories, and to conduct visits to and inspections of the territories themselves.[12] Through the operation of this system all of the original trust territories, with the exception of New Guinea and the Trust Territory of the Pacific Islands, had gained their independence by early 1968.

While the U.N. trusteeship system was essentially an improved version of the League mandates, the truly "striking innovation"[13] in this area affected by the Charter was the provisions of Chapter XI and, more specifically, the provisions of Article 73. In this article the members of the United Nations, including those administering dependent territories, committed themselves to the proposition that "interests of the inhabitants of these territories are paramount," and accepted as

> . . . a sacred trust the obligation to promote to the utmost . . . the well-being of the inhabitants . . . to develop self government, to take due account of the political aspirations of the peoples, and to assist them in the progressive development of their free political institutions, according to the particular circumstances of each territory and its people. . . .

The administering powers further agreed to transmit regularly to the Secretary General statistical reports on the economic, social and educational conditions in their respective dependent territories.

The covenant's "sacred trust" was thus proclaimed to embrace not only the people of former enemy territories but, indeed, to embrace the people of all dependent territories. The colonial powers had stated their formal recognition of the principle that their own, long-held colonial possessions were now wards of the international community as a whole, and that the objective of their administrations, at least in the eyes of the international community, was to provide these people with such assistance as might be required for their ultimate exercise of the right of self-determination. Significantly absent, however, was any institutionalized system to oversee the exercise of this "sacred trust" with respect to any of the non-trusteeship territories.

As noted previously, the United Nations trusteeship system has functioned so effectively that all but two of the original eleven trust territories have now gained their independence. Many explanations could be given for this, not the least of which could be that the territories involved were not long-term historical possessions of the administering powers but, rather, were former enemy territories of relatively recent acquisition. Also, it is obvious that the machinery of the Charter gave the international community as a whole a rather significant influence over these territories through the powers legislated to the Trusteeship Council.

In the first 15 years of the United Nations's operations, some 34 dependent territories, including 8 trusteeship and 22 non-trusteeship territories, had gained their independence.[14] Nevertheless, there remained at the end of 1960, 64 dependent territories under the administration of colonial powers.[15] While there had been major progress toward decolonization, it is quite apparent that with respect to the non-trusteeship dependencies, the progress was measurably slower than was the case with those under Trusteeship Council supervision. It was to speed up this process that the United Nations, augmented in 1960 with the admission to membership of 17 ex-colonial states, took such significant action that this year must be described as the watershed in the "rising tide of decolonization."[16]

In a dramatic address before the General Assembly on 23 September 1960, Nikita S. Khrushchev, then Chairman of the Council of Ministers of the U.S.S.R., stated that the time had come for "complete and final abolition of the colonial system in all its forms and manifestations," and he submitted for the consideration of the General Assembly a draft declaration calling for the granting of immediate independence to all trust and non-self-governing territories.[17] A modified Soviet proposal later submitted proclaimed that in the colonial territories "the swish of the overseer's lash is heard . . . [that] . . . heads fall under the executioner's axe," that all colonial countries must be granted their independence forthwith "and that all foreign bases in other states must be eliminated."[18] Throughout the debates which followed, Soviet spokesmen continued this type of vitriolic attack on all forms of "Western colonialism," giving particular and strident verbal attention to the subject of western military bases in foreign countries and western military alliances. Western spokesmen answered these attacks by accusing the Soviet Union, itself, of adopting a new form of colonialism which "had been imposed by force on people who had been free for centuries." They also made a specific point of stating their recognition of the aspirations of all people who did not presently enjoy a full measure of self-government and expressed a profound regret that the Soviet Union would undertake to "pervert for its own purposes the deep and genuine desires" of these peoples.[19]

Recognizing the urgent need for a resolution more moderate in tone than that submitted by the Soviet Union, and perhaps recognizing also the urgent need to attempt to remove U.N. decolonization efforts from the center of the East-West cold war struggle where it had been cast by the Soviets, 43 Afro-Asian nations collaborated in drafting a compromise resolution on this subject. This resolution was submitted to the General Assembly by Cambodia, and it was adopted on 19 December 1960, as General Assembly Resolution 1514 (XV), by a vote of 89 to 0 with nine nations, including all of the western colonial powers, abstaining.[20]

This declaration has been variously described as a "capstone to the U.N.'s efforts to supervise colonial regimes,"[21] as a kind of anticolonialism "magna carta,"[22] and as "almost an amendment to the Charter."[23] Certainly, all of these descriptions are accurate, since the resolution itself speaks in broader and yet more definite terms than has any similar document in history.[24] In its operative paragraphs it declared:

1. The subjection of peoples to alien domination and exploitation constitutes a denial of fundamental human rights, is contrary to the Charter of the United Nations and is an impediment to the promotion of world peace and cooperation.

2. All people have the right to self-determination; by virtue of that right they freely determine their political status and freely pursue their economic, social and cultural development.

3. Inadequacy of political, economic, social or educational preparedness should never serve as a pretext for delaying independence.

4. All armed action or repressive measures of all kinds directed against dependent peoples shall cease. . . .

5. Immediate steps shall be taken . . . to transfer all powers to the peoples of these territories, without any conditions or reservations, in accordance with their freely expressed will and desire, . . . in order to enable them to enjoy complete independence and freedom.

6. Any attempt aimed at the partial or total disruption of the national unity and the territorial integrity of a country is incompatible with the purposes and principles of the Charter of the United Nations.

7. All States shall observe faithfully and strictly the provisions of the
Charter of the United Nations, the Universal Declaration of Human
Rights, and the present Declaration on the basis of equality, respect
for the sovereign rights of all peoples and their territorial integrity.

Without a single dissenting vote, the General Assembly thus proclaimed
what must be regarded as an overwhelming international consensus that
the era of colonialism was past and that all of its remnants must give
way to the right of all people to self-determination.

While it is true that the General Assembly is not a lawmaking body,
that it can only recommend and not legislate, the overwhelming majority
by which this resolution was adopted and the fact that not even the
colonial powers against whom it was primarily directed dared vote against
it indicates the persuasive moral force that underlay it. Thus it must be
said that, technical legal arguments notwithstanding, the international
community regards it as a morally, and perhaps legally, defensible proposition that all peoples have a right to self-determination, which "demands
the speediest possible ending of all colonial relationships, and condemns
utterly any extension or reestablishment of colonial rule."[25]

The political lessons long taught by western philosophers and statesmen
had thus come back full circle, and the former pupils, now possessed of
organized moral and political strength in an international setting, were
reminding their former tutors in forceful terms of the lessons learned. It
does seem ironic, however, that the western nations have appeared to
abdicate their leading role in this effort to their cold war adversaries in
the Soviet Union.

Seizing the initiative again in the session of the General Assembly, of
26 September 1961, the Soviet Union complained that, despite the 1960
declaration, some 88 territories still remained under colonial domination,
that no steps had been taken to transfer administration to the indigenous
peoples, and that, further, "the colonialist powers' network of bases on
foreign soil was being used to hamper the liberation of colonial peoples
and jeopardize the independence of newly independent countries." The
Soviets again submitted a draft resolution for consideration.[26] It called, in
part, for the final and unconditional liquidation of colonialism by not later
than the end of 1962 and for the establishment of a special commission
to inquire into the situation with regard to the implementation of the
1960 declaration. A compromise resolution was again proposed by a group-
ing of Afro-Asian states, which, after considerable discussions repeating the

acrimony of the 1960 debates, was adopted by an overwhelming vote of 97 to 0 with only four abstentions.

Resolution 1654 (XVI) of 27 November 1961 reaffirmed the provisions of the declaration and called upon all states to take action "without further delay" to implement it. The resolution also established a special committee of 17 members, to be appointed by the President of the General Assembly, to inquire into the situation regarding implementation of the declaration and to make appropriate recommendations and suggestions.[27] In 1963, with the addition to its competence of matters involving the trust territories, this committee became the only U.N. body under the General Assembly which was concerned generally with all non-self-governing territories.[28]

In early 1962 the President of the General Assembly appointed the following states as members of the Special Committee: Australia, Cambodia, Ethiopia, India, Italy, Madagascar, Mali, Poland, Syria, Tanganyika, Tunisia, the U.S.S.R., the United Kingdom, the United States, Uruguay, Venezuela and Yugoslavia.[29] At the 17th session of the General Assembly, the membership of the Committee was expanded to a total of 24 by the addition of Bulgaria, Chile, Denmark, Iran, Iraq, Ivory Coast and Sierra Leone.[30]

With this composition it takes little imagination to envisage the philosophy which the Committee was to adopt and the course of action it was to follow. It does seem worthy of note that the Committee, from its outset, was weighed heavily against those powers which administered dependent territories. Of the twenty-four Committee members, twelve were ex-colonial territories, four were Soviet oriented and only three administering powers—Australia, the United Kingdom and the United States—were represented. New Zealand, which at the time continued to administer the Cook Islands and Niue and Tokelau Islands, was not even represented; nor were France and Portugal, both of whom continued to administer several dependent territories.

As would be expected from the composition of the Special Committee, it gave its initial attention to the African dependent territories, and the problems of these territories have continued to be foremost in the Committee's considerations. However in 1964 the three subcommittees were established generally for Africa and the eastern Indian Ocean, Asia and the Pacific Ocean, and the Atlantic and Caribbean areas and the Committee significantly broadened its activities. It was in this year that it first began to study closely the Pacific Island dependencies. Some 16 Pacific Island areas were considered. These areas were dispersed throughout the central and western Pacific, both above and below the equator, and comprised literally thousands of islands—from Pitcairn with a land area of only two square miles and a population of only 126, to Papua and New Guinea with land areas of over 180,000 square miles and a combined population in excess of two million. The Committee's task was further complicated by the fact that these island areas were administered by six separate administering powers—the United Kingdom, the United States, Australia, New Zealand, France, and Portugal.

Territory	Adm. Power	Area (sq. mi.)	Population
Timor	Portugal	7,332	500,000
Brunei	United Kingdom	2,226	104,000
Fiji	United Kingdom	7,055	400,000
Cook Island	New Zealand	93	18,500
Niue	New Zealand	100	4,900
Tokelau	New Zealand	4	1,900
Nauru	Australia	8	4,000
Papua	Australia	87,540	500,000
New Guinea	Australia	93,000	1,500,000
American Samoa	United States	76	20,000
Guam	United States	209	50,000
Trust Territory of the Pacific Islands	United States	687	90,000
New Hebrides	United Kingdom/France	5,700	60,000
Gilbert/Ellice	United Kingdom	369	47,000
Solomons	United Kingdom	11,500	130,000
Pitcairn	United Kingdom	2	126

The Committee met almost continuously during 1964, considering most of the non-self-governing territories in the Pacific in some detail. Reports were submitted to the General Assembly covering each of the territories considered, and recommendations were made concerning each territory. Although these differed in detail one from the other, the same general thread ran through them all—the Committee's insistence that progress toward self-determination in all of the territories was too slow and that the people of each of these areas should be given the earliest opportunity to express their wishes with regard to their future status "in accordance with well established democratic processes under United Nations supervision." The reports were generally accompanied by reservations from the administering powers who felt either that they did not accurately reflect the conditions in the territory, that proposed visits to some of the territories were outside the Committee's competence, or that progress toward self-determination was entirely consistent with the needs and desires of the local populations.[31]

Two aspects of the 1964 Committee reports deserve special consideration: (1) the apparent conflict between the Trusteeship Council and the heavily oriented anti-colonialism of the Special Committee; and (2) the growing determination of the Special Committee that complete independence must be the goal sought for all dependent peoples, regardless of their own needs or of their possible future independent viability.

Concerning the first of these, the Trusteeship Council's reports to the General Assembly, while urging the administering powers to continue their efforts leading toward self determination in their respective territories, did express general satisfaction with the political procedures being implemented in each of them.[32] With respect to the U.S. administered Trust Territory of the Pacific Islands, the Council took special note of the report of its visiting mission that "no fully matured opinions" had yet developed in the territory concerning its political future. Further, it expressed the hope that the "future Congress of Micronesia would direct its attention to all the possibilities—from independence to all other options—which lay open for the future of the Territory."[33]

The Trusteeship Council's reports were in marked contrast to the findings of the Committee of Twenty-four that the progress toward self-determination in the Trust Territory of the Pacific Islands "did not fully meet the requirements of the Charter" and of the 1960 declaration and that progress in New Guinea and Nauru "had been slow and adequate steps had not yet been taken."[34]

Another area of conflict arose in the Special Committee's proposal to send its own visiting mission to the Trust Territory of the Pacific Islands. Strenuous U.S. objection was voiced to such a visit since it was considered that visiting missions to trust territories were the peculiar province of the Trusteeship Council and were, hence, outside the competence of the Special Committee. This objection was overruled by the Committee by what had become an almost characteristic voting pattern of sixteen to five with three abstentions.

It is worth noting, also, that in its 1964 report on the Trust Territory of the Pacific Islands, the Trusteeship Council expressed an approval of several ultimate solutions for a dependent territory extending from "independence to all other options." The Special Committee, on the other hand, had from the beginning steadfastly opted for complete independence as the only acceptable goal. While this may not be readily apparent on the face of the Committee's reports, it does become clearer when one notes that the Committee consistently refers only to the 1960 declaration which speaks in terms of "complete independence." The two bodies consistently ignored one another, and perhaps more pertinent, they both ignored the General Assembly Resolution which proclaims the Assembly's understanding of the term "self-determination." On 15 December 1960, only one day after the 1960 declaration was adopted, the General Assembly adopted Resolution 1541 (XV), which states: "A Non-Self-Governing Territory can be said to have reached a full measure of self-government by: (a) Emergence as a sovereign independent state; (b) Free association with an independent state; or (c) Integration with an independent state."[35] By ignoring this resolution in its entirety and by consistently reiterating only the theme of the 1960 declaration, the Committee clearly indicated an unwillingness to accept any status short of "complete independence" as a satisfactory conclusion of the self-determination process. This absolute demand sometimes overrode the interests of the people involved, and this was illustrated by the results of a plebiscite in 1965 in which the Cook Islanders elected free association with New Zealand rather than complete independence.[36]

Another activity of the Committee, which first became apparent in 1964, is its announced determination to carry another of the declaration's principles to extreme lengths, that no reason—smallness, isolation, inadequate political, economic, social or educational preparation—should impede the granting of independence. In its 1964 reports on the small island territories, the Committee declared that, regardless of their size, the "provisions of the Declaration were fully applicable to . . . [them] . . . and that appropriate measures to this end should be taken without delay."

The nonsensical situation which this sort of thinking can bring about is demonstrated by the fact that in January 1968 the Territory of Nauru, with a land area of only eight square miles and a total population of only 4000 persons, became an independent, sovereign state.[37]

The Committee's 1965 proceedings brought forth once again what was then becoming a familiar refrain. The Soviet Union, supported by its Communist friends and by most of the former colonial states, continued to condemn the slowness of the pace toward independence, and for the first time the Soviet Union went on record as opposing any sort of merger between the administering powers and their dependent territories.[38] More significantly, however, the U.S.S.R. used the Committee as a vehicle to continue its cold war assault on western military bases on foreign soil, and particularly to condemn those located in dependent territories. As a result of the Committee's recommendations, a draft resolution was adopted by the General Assembly's Fourth Committee which stated that the existence of military bases in dependent territories "constituted an obstacle to the freedom and idependence of these territories" and called upon the administering powers to dismantle them. These provisions were approved by a forty-eight to thirty-seven affirmative vote in the General Assembly, but, they were rejected since they did not receive the two-thirds majority required for passing an "important question," which the President of the Assembly considered them to be. This procedural ruling was to obtain for less than one month, however, and on 20 December 1965 a U.S. objection based on this point was overruled. By a simple majority the General Assembly adopted Resolution 2105 (XX), requesting the "colonial Powers to dismantle their military bases in colonial Territories and to refrain from establishing new ones."[39]

The conflict between the Special Committee and the Trusteeship Council became more obvious in 1965. With respect to the three remaining trust territories, the Trusteeship Council again indicated general satisfaction with the progress being made. In coming to these conclusions, the Council had specifically rejected Soviet proposals which would have condemned the administering powers' discharge of their trusts.[40] The Special Committee, however, reported to the General Assembly in almost the same critical terms which had been rejected by the Trusteeship Council. The voting strength of the anti-colonialist bloc in the General Assembly was clearly illustrated by the adoption of certain resolutions. The General Assembly only took note of the conclusions of the Trusteeship Council while it affirmatively endorsed "the recommendations and conclusions of the Special Committee."

This vote gave credence to the belief that left little doubt that, at least as far as the General Assembly was concerned, the Special Committee reflected the General Assembly's sympathies and would probably be used as the U.N.'s principal anti-colonialist tool, regardless of the provisions of the Charter.

This has certainly been the case since 1965. A procedure seems to have been adopted under which subcommittees, without even "token representation" of the administering powers, have provided critical reports to the Committee which then, almost verbatim, endorsed the subcommittee's criticism and forwarded it to the General Assembly which also has accepted them. This has resulted in resolutions adopted by the General

Assembly during both 1966 and 1967[41] which have, in ever more strident language, condemned the "negative attitude" of the administering powers and their "repression of colonial peoples," reasserted that colonialism is "incompatible with the Charter," reiterated that "the establishment of military bases and installations in these territories is incompatible with the purposes and principles of the Charter . . . and of General Assembly Resolution 1514 (XV)." The General Assembly has requested that existing military installations be dismantled; and, finally, have deplored the refusal of the administering powers to admit missions of committee members to the dependent territories and requested that such missions be accepted.

Both the Committee's and the General Assembly's debates which preceded the above resolutions demonstrate that the former colonial states, have been steered by the U.S.S.R. into attacks on the western states and particularly on the United States. Thus, the former colonial states' initial reluctance to enter this "second cold war" has broken down. The debates on the military bases issue provide evidence of this. At the beginning of its 1967 sessions, the Committee heard the Soviet Representative, supported by many other members, condemn the existence of military bases in all dependent territories and state that "the utilization of military bases on Guam . . . showed that they created an obstacle to independence."[42] The Soviet Union, through the Committee forum in 1967, urged that the United States should be requested to dismantle its military bases in the Trust Territory of the Pacific Islands, the provisions of the strategic trusteeship agreement notwithstanding.[43] In May of 1967 letters were dispatched to each of the administering powers asking for information on their military activities in the territories under their administration. In July and August 1967 replies were received from Australia, New Zealand, the United Kingdom and the United States. None were willing to provide such information, contending that their obligation to provide information on their territories was subject to security limitations and that the subcommittee had no right to ask for this type of information from them. As might be expected, this brought forth a rash of criticism of the Western Powers who, it was said, had the temerity to "challenge the Committee's right to information" and whose real purpose was to use their military bases "against freedom loving people."[44]

The Committee's continued insistence on immediate implementation of the 1960 declaration and their continued rejection of any attempts by the administering powers to demonstrate that progress toward self-determination in their respective territories was in the best interests of the local population led the U.S. Representative to complain bitterly in early 1968 about what were termed "serious defects in the Committee's methods of work."[45] He stated that the stereotyped and persistent call for immediate independence was improper since "it was doubtful if independence was feasible" for all of them. He also deplored the breakdown in communications within the Committee which frequently led to the exclusion of representatives of the administering powers when resolutions were being drafted which were of particular concern to them. He ended his presentation with the startling announcement that:

> . . . [In] view of the Committee's methods of work and the difficulties they have created for his delegation, the United States questioned whether any purpose would be achieved by further participation in the work of the Committee and was considering withdrawal. After consulting with other delegations, however, his delegation had decided to defer its decision on that question.

The United Kingdom also made strong complaints about the Committee's methods of work and provided suggestions for their change as well as for changes in the Committee's organization.[46]

The ensuing debates saw, not an attempt by the Committee to structure its activities with a purpose of achieving more progress towards its goal by diplomatic means, but, rather, a strident renewal of cold war invective. The Soviet Representative attacked the United States as "relentlessly undermining the efforts of the United Nations to end oppression . . . [and] . . . attempting to crush the people of Vietnam under the force of arms." He accused the United States of occupying for many years "a number of Territories in the Pacific . . . and transforming them into air and naval bases and instruments of its struggle against dependent peoples."[47] Syria said that the United States and the United Kingdom were trying to "ridicule the Committee and discredit it." Yugoslavia and India contended that the real difficulty was not the Committee's methods, but the refusal on the part of the administering powers to cooperate. Bulgaria and Poland supported these criticisms and added their own charges of "perpetuating the colonialist yoke," "ruthless foreign exploitation," and the use of these small territories "as sites for military bases" through which to further their aggressive purposes. Finally, the Representative of Mali echoed the Communist line by arguing that the "subtle attempts" to restrict the Committee's activities were "only an extension of the desperate . . . [death throes] . . . offensive unleashed by the coalition of reactionary neocolonialist and imperialist forces."[48]

With these stinging and bitter accusations at the beginning of the 1968 Committee sessions, the Communist states, with support from the former colonial states, gave warning that they intended to utilize the anti-colonialist cause to its full measure in their attacks on the United States. The U.S. bases on Guam drew particularly extensive condemnation. It was contended that they were typical examples of how the existence of military installations were having a negative effect "not only on the liberation of their people, but also on international relations in general," and that they were being used "for intervention and aggression against the people of Viet-Nam."[49] Guam was described as "nothing but a vast military base . . . [whose] . . . population had been inducted into the foreign army,"[50] and the United States was accused of using the islands of the Trust Territory of the Pacific Islands as missile and air bases and of planning a further expansion of its military activities in that area. Australia was attacked for what was said to be "military preparations . . . [in Papua and New Guinea] . . . for the conduct of the aggressive war in Viet Nam and for the direct induction of indigenous soldiers into that war."[51]

During these 1968 proceedings the Representative of the Soviet Union spelled out succinctly what lay behind the Soviet offensive. In one of his most biting attacks to date, he said on 25 June 1968:[52]

> The information before the Committee showed that the strategic significance of small Territories, especially islands, had increased, because they could be used for supporting far-reaching military operations. That was particularly true of the island of Guam, a United States Colony in the Pacific Ocean, which had been turned into a military fortress . . . [T]he military headquarters of the region, an American Naval Base at Apra Harbour, the Agana Naval Air Station and the Anderson Air Force Base were on Guam. Some 38,500 servicemen and their dependents had been attached to these bases in 1967. The Anderson Air Force Base was the staging point from which the B-52 bombers were used for the aggressive war against the Viet-Namese people who were battling for their freedom and independence . . . and Guam was being used . . . for Polaris submarines which were patrolling Chinese waters.

It does seem obvious, however, that the majority of the Committee has permitted its purpose to be converted from that of an international overseer of the self-determination process into that of a forum for propaganda assaults on the U.S. presence in Southeast Asia and in the Pacific Ocean area in general. What the attitude of the United States should be toward the Committee's work in the face of such unreasoning assaults is a matter which deserves to be given careful consideration.

There is no question but that the yearning of the world's peoples for control over their own political destinies is a fact of 20th century life which must be intelligently dealt with by the present administering powers, the dependent peoples themselves, and the international community as a whole. There also seems to be little doubt that the activities of the United Nations, to date, both in the Trusteeship Council and in the Special Committee of 24, have given considerable momentum to the self-determination process. The independence of Nauru and the U.S. announcement of a planned 1972 plebiscite in the Trust Territory of the Pacific Islands are only the most recent evidence of the effect of international pressure through these U.N. organs. What seems to be lacking in the process, however, at least as viewed by a majority of the members of the United Nations, is the realization that the continued insistence on "complete independence" as the only acceptable goal of the self-determination process can, and undoubtedly will, lead to the same type of fragmented, nonviable, political picture in the Pacific as that which created world tensions in the 19th century. Certainly the anti-colonialists are right when they describe the struggle for colonial empires as a source of world conflict which can lead to war, and if this type of conflict is to be avoided in the future, it seems essential that conditions should not be recreated which could lead to the same type of instability and struggle.

This is not to say that the peoples of any particular Pacific Island territory should not be enabled to opt for complete freedom, unassociated with any stronger power, if it is their desire to do so. It *is* to say that these peoples should not be pushed into such an option if it is really not in their best interests, as judged by themselves.

Part I   Melanesia

2 / Trust Territories of Melanesia

David Glenn Wilson,

Commander, United States Navy

Immediately following World War II, the victorious powers were faced with the problem of the administration of the non-self-governing islands previously occupied by the Japanese forces. The United Nations ultimately resolved the issue by establishing a Trusteeship Council charged with the administration and supervision of these and certain other specified territories. This chapter will be concerned with those territories south of the equator that were placed in a trust status by the United Nations. It analyzes the historical background of the territories under consideration, reviews the progress made toward the advancement of the subject inhabitants and attempts to forecast the future relationship between these territories as members of the world community.

Though the concept of trusteeship was not formally codified until the United Nations Charter in 1946, the principle is much older. Queen Isabella of Spain acknowledged that more advanced powers have a special duty with respect to the welfare and advancement of more backward peoples, and she specifically spoke out on behalf of the exploited Indians in Central and South America. In 1783, Edmund Burke defined the relationship that should exist between British traders in India as a "trust" to be exercised for the welfare of the Indians. The United States, in 1900, described the Philippine Islands as "an unsought trust which should be unselfishly discharged." And more recently, the mandates system, established by the League of Nations after World War I, was conceived as a mechanism of trusteeship for backward and impoverished peoples.

On 13 December 1946, the General Assembly of the United Nations approved the final draft resolutions placing under trusteeship the territories previously held as League of Nations mandates. This action resulted in, among other things, the establishment in the South Pacific of the Trust Territories of New Guinea, Nauru Island and Western Samoa. The concept of trusteeship was some one hundred and fifty years old at that time. However, the basic foundation for the lines of authority and administration of the newly formed territories can be traced almost directly to more immediate factors; namely to the colonial alignment within the area at the outbreak of World War I, the strategic fears generated by the realignment after that war, and the shortcomings of the League of Nations in the administration of those territories prior to World War II.[1]

At the outbreak of World War I Germany had extensive island holdings in the Pacific. These included the Marshalls, the Carolines, the Palaus and the Marianas north of the equator and Kaiser Wilhelmsland (now North-East New Guinea), the Bismarck Archipelago, Western Samoa, and the Island of Nauru south of the equator. Shortly after the initiation of hostilities in Europe, the Japanese moved south and east into the German islands in support of the Anglo-Japanese Alliance while the Australians and New Zealanders moved north and east in response to an Imperial request to seize the German wireless stations in the Pacific.[2]

The Australians, after occupying New Britain and Bougainville in the Bismarck Archipelago, proceeded to Yap to secure the German facility there. Upon arrival they found that Japanese forces were firmly entrenched. This rapid movement southward by the Japanese, combined with a need to secure the German holdings more nearly adjacent to the Japanese mainland led to a natural and ultimately British-dictated policy of United Kingdom control of the islands south of the equator and a toleration of Japanese supremacy to the north. At the outbreak of hostilities it was not intended that Japan should supersede Germany in the islands, but the rapidity of the Japanese movement and the totality of their control dictated that the solution, with respect to ultimate control, be postponed until more stable times. To allay the apprehensions of the United States about having an apparently expansionistic Japan occupying a strong flanking position on its routes to the Philippines, both London and Tokyo indicated that Japan had no intention of holding these islands after the war.[3] Australia and New Zealand continued their consolidation efforts within their areas of constraint and the German influence in the Pacific was promptly eliminated. Japan assumed absolute control to the north of the equator and United Kingdom forces controlled all of the strongholds previously held by the Germans south of the equator.

As the war neared conclusion it became apparent that the Japanese did not intend to withdraw from the former German islands. This, coupled with Japanese expansion on the Asian mainland, caused considerable concern in the United States. The grave potential inherent in the trend was also detected by the British historian, Guy Scholefield, who wrote:

> Japan's claim to the small islands north of the equator is certain to be sanctioned out of appreciation for Japanese loyalty to the cause of the Allies. Nevertheless, this first steppingout of the Asiatic power into far outposts in the Pacific is an entirely new departure, and it cannot fail to contain the seeds of new misgivings for the future.[4]

It was not until 1918, when the Bolsheviks opened the imperial Russian Archives, that the Japanese plan for perpetual hegemony over the German islands in Micronesia was publicly confirmed. The records revealed that Britain, Russia and France had entered into a secret agreement with Japan in 1917 that guaranteed joint support for Japanese claims in the Pacific in return for anti-submarine support in the Mediterranean. The treaty that evolved further provided for Japanese support of British, Australian, and New Zealand claims to permanent possession of the German territories south of the equator.[5]

While the Australians were aware of the secret agreement with Japan, they were not given a voice in the proceedings and could only insist that their rights south of the equator be equally guaranteed. There is evidence to indicate that some respected elements in Australia did not consider Japan a threat at all and found ". . . no reason why the British Empire, in hearty cooperation with the United States and Japan, should not control the Pacific to the advantage of everybody concerned."[6] This author, in fact, saw the Japanese as a constant and unfaltering ally in their dealings with all of the nations arrayed against Germany.

There appeared, however, to be a strong and prevalent fear in Australia of seeing the territories returned to Germany after the war. The most vocal and dominant exponent of the permanent expulsion of Germany from the Pacific was Australian Prime Minister William Hughes, a man described as "an Australian Theseus fighting the German Minotaur."[7] This fiery proponent of total victory toured the United Kingdom during 1916 and gathered an impressive following, including Lloyd George, the Northcliffes and the extreme militarists in the British Isles.[8]

The views of Hughes were amplified by Sir Joseph Cook and Sir William MacGregor who put forth the premise that Australia did not desire to retain the German colonies from any lust for new and additional territory, but rather as a security against "bad neighbors" and it was never indicated that they suspected any country other than Germany of being a potentially bad neighbor.[9]

The Prime Minister of England, Lloyd George, during the latter days of 1917, expressed a personal distaste for ". . . stripping Germany of all of the backward territories she had done much to open out and to equip."[10] Faced, however, with the secret wartime agreements concerning the disposition of the Pacific colonies and a unanimous fear voiced by spokesmen from South Africa to representatives from New Zealand of again having German neighbors, he acceded to a program to prevent the return of the German colonies.

The American view with respect to the ultimate disposition of the German colonies was enmeshed in the overall, grand scheme of President Wilson to form a League of Nations designed to make the world safe for democracy.[11] Consequently, when the victorious powers met in Versailles on 28 June 1919 not a voice was raised in favor of restoring the German colonies. Article 119 was quickly adopted which states: "Germany renounces in favour of the Principal Allied and Associated Powers all her rights and titles over her overseas possessions."[12] This article succinctly announced that Germany would no longer control her former overseas possessions, but left the responsibility for the disposition and administration of those possession to the proposed League of Nations.

Lloyd George, in his memoirs, indicates that President Wilson, had a highly idealistic view as to what the world should be like under the League, but that he had formulated no practical plans as to how to resolve the question of the German colonies. Prime Minister J. C. Smuts of South Africa had submitted a proposal that the League of Nations serve as a trustee, with mandatories nominated by the League to undertake the duties of administration. When Wilson was approached to approve the mandates system however, it appeared that the opposition to such proposal would be overpowering. Debate and discussion of the concept had even led the author of the proposal to oppose it. Lloyd George expressed the opinion that only he and President Wilson were in favor and it appeared that no solution would be found to the problem. The opinion expressed by Hughes was generally shared by the other powers located geographically adjacent to the former German colonies. He stated:

As Mr. Lloyd George has pointed out, part of the country . . . (New Guinea) . . . was under Australian administration, and Australian laws were current there. Control by the League of Nations would lead to confusion of authority, which could only be harmful. If the mandatory were to exercise real authority, its policy would have to be directed, presumably, by the League of Nations. In this case the mandatory would be so overwhelmingly superior in power to Australia that Australian authority would be completely overshadowed. The mandatory, as it were, would be living in a mansion and Australia in a cottage. Any strong power controlling New Guinea controlled Australia. . . . The security of Australia would threaten no one. No State would suffer if Australia were safe, Australia alone would suffer if she were not.[13]

Other dynamic and thought provoking speeches were given by the representatives of South Africa, New Zealand and France, all of whom favored annexation of the colonies. It was apparent that agreement was far off, tempers were taut, and the conference was in jeopardy. It was adjourned for two days during which time Lloyd George, in conference with Dominion spokesmen, devised a system of mandatories that would recognize three classes of mandates.[14]

A MANDATES. Certain communities formerly belonging to the Turkish Empire have reached a stage of development where their existence as independent nations can be provisionally recognized subject to the rendering of administrative advice and assistance by a Mandatory until such time as they are able to stand alone. . . .

B MANDATES. Other peoples, especially those of Central Africa, are at such a stage that the Mandatory must be responsible for the administration of the territory under conditions which will guarantee freedom of conscience and religion, subject only to the maintenance of public order and morals, the prohibition of abuses such as the slave trade, the arms traffic and the liquor traffic, etc.

C MANDATES. There are territories, such as Southwest Africa and certain of the South Pacific Islands, which, owing to the sparseness of their population, or their small size, or their remoteness from the centres of civilization, or their geographical contiguity to the territory of the Mandatory, and other circumstances, can be best administered under the laws of the Mandatory as integral portions of its territory, subject to the safeguards above-mentioned in the interests of the indigenous populations.[15]

These provisions, along with general administration guidelines, were ultimately adopted as Article 22 of the Covenant to the League of Nations. They were not adopted, however, before a considerable amount of heated debate; an example of which was related in the Lloyd George memoirs:

... Mr. Hughes having stated his case against subjecting to a mandate the islands conquered by Australia, President Wilson pulled him up sharply and proceeded to address him personally in what I would describe as a heated allocution rather than an appeal. He dwelt on the seriousness of defying world opinion on this subject. Mr. Hughes, who listened intently, with his hand cupped around his ear so as not to miss a word, indicated at the end that he was still of the same opinion. Whereupon the President asked him slowly and solemnly: "Mr. Hughes, am I to understand that if the whole civilized world asks Australia to agree to a mandate in respect of these islands, Australia is prepared still to defy the appeal of the whole civilized world?" Mr. Hughes answered: "That's about the size of it, President Wilson." Mr. Massey (New Zealand) grunted his assent of this abrupt defiance.[16]

This belligerent attitude prevailed momentarily and threatened to destroy the conference. It was only through the very diplomatic speech subsequently given by General Botha of South Africa that order was returned to the meeting and agreement was reached for the adoption of the article regarding the mandatories. All of the islands south of the equator were ultimately declared to be Class C mandates with Australia the mandatory for German New Guinea and the islands of the Bismarck Archipelago, New Zealand the mandatory for Western Samoa and the British Empire specified as the mandatory for the island of Nauru. The former Micronesian islands of Germany were also declared to be Class C mandates with Japan as the mandatory.

The period immediately subsequent to the resolution of the disposition of the mandated territories found Australia generally complacent internationally, though there was an undercurrent of suspicion with respect to the Japanese purposes and activities in the Micronesian islands.[17] This anxiety was further heightened by the prospect of termination of the Anglo-Japanese treaty which the Australians believed had a moderating effect upon Japanese aggressive tendencies.

The major interests of the Australian and New Zealand governments were internal development, expansion of the economy (including that of the territories), and support of the British buildup in Singapore.

In no island group did the European masters envision a future which included the establishment or reestablishment of native sovereignty. Any ideas of the paramountcy of the native interest were bounded by the idea that the natives obviously required tutelage—

including the tutelage of wage labor under Europeans—for many
years to come; it seemed fantastically improbable that native sovereignty in the twentieth century could be sustained any more successfully than in the nineteenth century.[18]

New Guinea, in particular, was largely unexplored and underdeveloped,
except near the coast. The copra output was gradually increased and
several rich gold deposits were discovered. The total output from all
sources, however, was still insufficient to permit any significant improvement in the social and economic conditions of the natives. The Mandates
Commission issued critical complaints to Australia with respect to labor
practices, lack of education of the natives and failure to provide meaningful
health services. The administration reviewed policies but up until the outbreak of World War II had not done anything to correct the deficiencies.

Soon after the attack by Japan upon Pearl Harbor, the Japanese forces
invaded the islands off New Guinea. The civil administration of the mandate was moved from Rabaul to Port Morseby in Papua. It appeared at
the time that the Japanese moves into the Solomons and Rabaul was an
immediate effort to invade Australia and New Zealand. Only after the war
could it be determined that these moves were only part of an effort by
Japan to protect its southern flanks from a United States countermove.[19]
The Japanese subsequently placed an expeditionary force ashore in New
Guinea and offensive operations continued in this area through 1944.

A second mandated territory, Nauru Island, was also destined to be
occupied by the Japanese. It had been administered by the Australians by
mutual agreement of the United Kingdom, Australia and New Zealand.
This island, lying twenty-six miles south of the equator, contained the
richest deposit of phosphate in the Pacific and represented a significant
resource for the power executing control over exploitation. It was estimated
that in 1920 fully 86% of the twelve-square-mile island was phosphate
bearing. The United Kingdom bought out the mineral rights to the island
from a German firm in 1919 and continued the mining operation that the
Germans had started. The question was raised before the Mandate Commission as to whether such sole right to the development of the natural
resources of a mandated territory was fully in keeping with the spirit of
the mission of the mandatory. The issue was dropped when it was determined that the purchase of the mining rights had been made by the
British prior to the mandate's having been conferred.[20] Under the terms
of administration of the island, the native Nauruans were prevented by
law from being induced to work in the mines. It appeared as if most of

them preferred to live from the royalties paid and distributed among them by the mining firm. Chinese coolies were imported to work the mines and by 1930 they were as numerous as the native inhabitants of the island. Nothing of international consequence occurred in Nauru during the mandate years except that the island continued to decrease in size as a result of the mining operations. The Japanese occupied the island from 1942–1945 and continued to exploit the natural resources.

The third mandated territory in the South Pacific, Western Samoa, was the only one relatively untouched by World War II. When the future of the German colonies had been decided after World War I, ". . . the New Zealanders were with regard to Western Samoa as much frustrated annexationists as the Australians were with regard to New Guinea or the Japanese with regard to Micronesia."[21] What was particularly frustrating to New Zealand was the fact that the only motivation for any relationship, with Samoa was defensive and strategic. The task of serving as a mandatory was looked upon as a thankless and unrewarding endeavor. The general view among the New Zealanders was, however, that the native interest should be paramount.[22] Their constancy in this respect was certainly in the highest accord with the intent of the mandate, stemming to some degree, no doubt, from the general belief that they had historically had a special gift for dealing with Polynesians. During the period of the mandate, the population and productivity increased and general welfare of the Samoans improved. Limited self-rule was introduced in 1923, and highly competitive political factions developed, leading to reckless demonstrations in 1929. The islands were geographically removed from the main arena of World War II. It was apparent, however, throughout this period, that the roots of discontent were deep and that the political makeup of the mandate system was destined to change.

As early as April of 1939 the leaders of Australia and New Zealand had acknowledged that their countries ". . . have primary responsibilities and primary risks . . ." in the southwest Pacific.[23] This realization led them to attempt to develop regional security arrangements that would strengthen their ability to meet those responsibilities and minimize those risks. The Australian Minister for External Affairs expressed his nation's concern and sentiment with respect to the issue in April 1943:[24]

> They reckon ill who leave the Pacific out of account. In point of
> fact, security must be universal or everyone will be insecure. This does

not mean, however, that within a system of general world security there will not be ample scope for the development of regional arrangements both for the purpose of the preservation of that security and for the handling of ordered change within that region.

When an adequate general plan is prepared for security against aggression, the United Nations in the Pacific will have to be assured of their own security. In this respect Australia will naturally regard as of crucial importance to its own security the arc of islands laying to the North and North-east of our continent . . . and will be vitally concerned as to who shall live in, develop, and control these areas so vital to her security from aggression.

As World War II continued and it became increasingly apparent that the Allied Powers were on the verge of defeating Japan, the governments of Australia and New Zealand entered into a highly controversial agreement designed to protect their interests in the postwar settlement with Japan. The agreement was known as the "ANZAC Pact" and was signed on 21 January 1944. It established procedures for mutual consultation between the two countries in such areas as defense and external policy affecting the Pacific. More significantly, it announced to the world that Australia and New Zealand claimed the "right" to representation at the highest level on all armistice-planning and executive bodies. It further stipulated that the ultimate disposition of enemy territories in the Pacific should be effected only with the agreement of Australia and New Zealand. To these mildly antagonistic claims, the signatories added:

> Article 13. The two Governments agree that, within the framework of a general system of world security, a regional zone of defense comprising the Southwest and South Pacific areas *shall* be established and that this zone should be based on Australia and New Zealand, stretching through the arc of islands north and northeast of Australia, to Western Samoa and Cook Islands.

> Article 16. The two Governments accept as a recognized principle of international practice that the construction and use, in time of war, by any power of naval, military or air installations, in any territory under the sovereignty or control of another power, does not, in itself, afford any basis for territorial claims or rights of soverignty or control after the conclusion of hostilities.[25]

The tone and content of the "ANZAC Pact" was duly noted by the major allied powers and caused some degree of consternation, particularly among American military leaders who were formulating a postwar national security plan at that time. Article 16 clearly implied that the bases devel-

oped in the South Pacific by the United States would probably be un-
available for continued use after the war if the ANZAC agreement were
recognized as valid. Of particular concern to the United States Navy was
the future status of the base at Manus Island, a part of the mandated
territory of New Guinea. Upon being approached by the United States
with a recommendation that the Manus base be retained by the U.S., the
Australian Minister for External Affairs would discuss only joint use of
the base and then only in the context of reciprocity with respect to
Australian use of other U.S. bases in the region.[26] This adamant stand on
the part of the Australians threatened to destroy all of the mutual trust
and confidence that had been developed through three years of harmoni-
ous relations between the two allies. It was believed by the Australians,
however, ". . . that Australia and New Zealand have taken to heart the
bitter experiences resulting in the failure to achieve collective security and
the international order which must be based on security . . ." and that
they would follow the course of collective security regardless of the sensi-
tivities of their closest Ally.[27] It was clear that the disasters of 1942 in
southeast Asia had convinced the Australian Government that the Pacific
had become a sphere of vital interest, direct peril, special responsibility,
and that it required detailed concern for the future power alignment in
the region.[28]

After the conclusion of hostilities in the Pacific, the Australian Government intensified its efforts to enter into a mutual security pact with the
United States based upon reciprocal use of bases throughout the entire
region. The United States was unwilling to conclude an agreement for
several reasons. First, it was heavily involved in European recovery and
defense and was reluctant to assume further commitments in the Pacific.
Additionally, there were indications given by the Department of the Navy
that the American strategic perimeter was redefined to be based at Manila
rather than Manus Island. Finally, the Australian formula for reciprocal
and joint use of bases was rejected as unacceptable to the United States.[29]

Although the United States had shown little desire to enter into a
mutually acceptable collective security arrangement with Australia and
New Zealand during the 1944–1945 period, it had continued to show
interest in the administering of New Zealand Mandated Territory of
Samoa and the British Territory of Christmas Island as well as the Manus
Island complex. Under American pressure the Australian delegation thus
arrived at the Charter Conference of the United Nations at San Francisco
in April 1945.

The Australian delegation was led by Dr. Herbert Vere Evatt, who, like his predecessor to the League of Nations, Prime Minister Hughes, brought a dynamic personality and a passionate drive to the conference. He brought a strong conviction that the rights and security of the "little powers" must be protected. One of the areas of concern to his Government was the ". . . maladministration of neighboring colonial territories . . ." by the administering powers.[30] An additional concern was the potential encroachment of the large powers upon the small powers, as he visualized was possible with respect to Manus Island. His Government had strongly endorsed the principle of "trusteeship" in the "ANZAC Pact" and he saw trusteeship as a potential vehicle to ensure the welfare and advancement of dependent and underdeveloped territories as well as to protect the former mandates from being removed from Australian control. He, along with the New Zealand Minister for External Affairs, Mr. Peter Fraser, led the forces that introduced the concept of trusteeship into the conference, despite the fact that it had been deliberately deleted from the Dumbarton Oaks draft which formed the foundation for the conference.[31]

The following year the General Assembly approved an Australian proposal establishing as a trust of Australia the mandated territory of New Guinea. Article 4 of the agreement provides that Australia will be responsible for the peace, order, good government and defense of the territory, and for this purpose will have the same powers of legislation, administration and jurisdiction in and over the territory as if it were an integral part of Australia, and will be entitled to apply to the territory, subject to such modification as it seems desirable, such laws of the Commonwealth of Australia as it seems appropriate to the needs and conditions of the territory. An additional article provides that Australia will decide what international agreements and recommendations of the United Nations agencies would be applied to New Guinea in the achievement of the basic objectives of the trusteeship system.[32]

The trusteeship agreement concerning New Guinea served as the model for the ultimate disposition of the remaining mandated territories in the South Pacific; Australia was designated as the agent of the British Empire in the administration of Nauru and New Zealand the trustee of Western Samoa. It can be debated whether Australia and New Zealand were motivated most by fear of national and regional security or by humanitarian considerations. The fact remains that trusteeship did serve to respond to either motivation and to both motivations.

The war had a pronounced impact upon New Guinea.[33] Much of the interior was opened up for the first time, the economy was wrecked, and the territory was without effective government from 1942–1945. The Labor Minister, E. J. Ward, was placed in charge of the administration of the territory, and set about to correct the deficiencies detected prior to the war. He issued the following policy statement:

> The government is not satisfied that sufficient interest had been taken in the territories prior to the Japanese invasion, or that adequate funds had been provided for their development and the advancement of the native inhabitants. Apart from the debt of gratitude that the people of Australia owe to the natives of the territory, the Government regards it as its bounden duty to further to the utmost the advancement of the natives, and considers that they can be achieved only by providing facilities for better health, better education, and for a greater participation by the natives in the wealth of their country and eventually in its government.[34]

The liberalized administration of New Guinea espoused by Mr. Ward was announced shortly after the United Nations Trusteeship Council became operational on 26 March 1947.

On 1 July 1949 the administrative union was formed between the Australian Territory of Papau and the U.N. Trust Territory of New Guinea with centralized administrative headquarters. This procedure had been previously defended in the United Nations and determined to be within the terms of the charter.[35]

The Trusteeship Council, in the early 1960s, began an intensive campaign, generally under the sponsorship of the U.S.S.R., to force Australia to establish firm time tables for independence of the New Guinea Trust Territory. Up until the present time the administration has resisted the pressure for a "hard schedule" but has voiced an opinion that ". . . Australia needed thirty to fifty years even to grant New Guinea conditional freedom."[36] It is generally conceded that the United Nations Special Committee on Ending Colonialism (Committee of Twenty-Four) will probably bring enough pressure to bear upon Australia to ensure that independence will be forced upon New Guinea long before the native population is prepared to cope with the problems of independence. One encouraging note was the fact that one of the first acts of the newly elected 1964 House of Assembly (a legislative body containing a native majority) was to indicate to the United Nations that it did not desire to be forced to accept independence prematurely. Certainly this last of the major trust territories appears to be trying to prepare for statehood in an orderly manner.

Nauru was made a trust territory at the same time as the other mandated territories. The Australians resumed the mining operations and reached a production rate of over 1,000,000 tons of phosphate a year. They established a dividend of one shilling, one pence, and were instrumental in raising the living standards of the Nauruans. It was estimated in 1960 that the phosphate would be worked out in forty years and the problem of the island's economic future was of concern to the islanders, the Australians and the Trusteeship Council.[37] The Trusteeship Council continued to pressure Australia to grant the island independence. This pressure was successfully resisted for a period of time with the help of New Zealand's defense of the status quo; ". . . Nauru can hardly be considered a nation in embryo and must necessarily have limited political horizons."[38] The extreme pressure finally succeeded, however, and Nauru became an independent state on 31 January 1968.[39] It did not seek to join the United Nations and is expected to associate politically and economically with Western Samoa in the near future.[40] In the meantime, the government of Nauru has formed a company to continue the mining of phosphate and the ultimate destiny of the islanders continues to be a question.

The strong evidence of a Samoan drive for national independence continued through the war years. When it was learned that New Zealand was preparing to enter into a trusteeship agreement, the Samoans petitioned the United Nations for immediate autonomy and self government with New Zealand functioning as sponsor. New Zealand supported this petition and a schedule was established which led to independence on 1 January 1962—the first of the Pacific island countries to regain "native sovereignty."[41] It is significant to note that Western Samoa, like Nauru later, did not apply for membership in the United Nations because it was too expensive. The country has continued to advance economically and has maintained close ties with New Zealand, who provides a nominal subsidy to the government. A disastrous hurricane in 1966 destroyed the agricultural crops for that year and forced the government to appeal to the United States for aid. When this request was turned down, the Prime Minister announced that he would seek aid from the U.S.S.R. if necessary in order to overcome the national disaster.[42] The Soviet newspaper *Izvestia* subsequently offered Russian scholarships to Samoan students. The future of this relationship is indefinite at this time though the expansionistic Soviet Navy is undoubtedly interested in developing friendly relations with a country with a fine harbor such as is found at Apia.

The review of the progress of the South Pacific Trust Territories indicates that the trustees, by and large, have functioned in accordance with the spirit of the charter in the promotion of political, economic, social and educational advancement of the inhabitants of the trust territories. Certainly New Zealand and Australia can take great pride in the performance of their trust in the last twenty years. Only time will tell if they will be permitted to continue to exercise leadership, stability and a peaceful influence in the continuing development of these territories.

3 / The Samoan Islands

George H. Dodenhoff,

Colonel, United States Marine Corps

with

W. D. Munsey,

Commander, United States Navy

Most of the Pacific Islands have been alternately coveted and neglected by most of the major world powers and were often the basis for disputes among them. Men and nations have been interested in the islands for a variety of reasons—religious, economic, or strategic, and very often the periods of interest brought more misery to the inhabitants of the islands than the periods of neglect.[1]

The Samoan Islands are part of the vast South Seas area known as Polynesia, which means "many islands." Most of Polynesia lies south of the equator. The Samoan archipelago is just east of the dividing line between Polynesia and Melanesia; farther to the west, Fiji is inhabited by dark haired Melanesians. The Samoan group is supposed to be the original home of the Polynesians in the Pacific before they made their way to Hawaii, Tahiti, New Zealand and other islands now inhabited by them. The traditional Hawaiki (homeland) of the Maoris and other legends has been identified with Savaii, the westernmost island. Of all the Polynesian dialects, the Samoan is considered to be the most archaic. The Samoans have a history of political squabbling and intertribal wars based on rival chieftainships extending back hundreds of years. But, no small group of Pacific Islands has seen more troublesome times, due largely to the intrusion of European powers, than Samoa.[2] Samoa has borne explorers, scientists, traders, missionaries, planters, and settlers, as well as all the agents of western governments variously arrayed for peace and war. Areas found to be climatically suitable for foreign occupation were colonized and native occupants were pushed aside with varying degrees of ruthlessness. Less inhabitable areas were pacified and then subjected to economic exploitation and political control.[3]

There is considerable literature about the Samoan Islands, including scientific works describing the land and traditions of the native people; cultural investigations of the ethnological migrations of the Polynesian people to the Samoan Islands, and historical documents and writings. However, many of these sources have strong political or missionary viewpoints and in considerable part pertain to the period prior to 1900. A number of official documents and records after that date, coupled with newspaper sources, provide a more current appraisal of the Samoan scene.

Samoa is the native name for the archipelago situated between latitudes 13°30′S and 14°30′S and longitudes 168°W and 173°W. It lies on the direct route between Auckland and the Hawaiian Islands, 2,276 miles to the northeast of Auckland. Savaii, the largest island, has an area of 703 square miles; Upolu, 10 miles to the east, is 430 square miles. Between these two islands are two islets the land mass of which makes the total area of Western Samoa about 1,200 square miles.[4]

Thirty-six miles east of Upolu in Western Samoa is the island of Tutuila in American Samoa, noted for its excellent harbor of Pago Pago, a location well known in history and fiction. Sixty miles further to the east is the Manua group of three islands: Tau, Olosego and Ofu. Continuing eastwardly 70 miles distant, is the uninhabited coral atoll, Rose Island. This entire group, together with Swain Island to the north, constitutes the territory of American Samoa. Including the uninhabited island of Aunuu there are seven islands in the group. The islands constitute a land mass of only 76.1 square miles, an area slightly larger than the District of Columbia and little more than one-half the size of the U.S. Virgin Islands.

Tutuila appealed to western eyes, and the sheltered inlet of Pago Pago was a frequent calling place for whalers and other vessels; it is often referred to as the finest harbor in the South Seas. Yet its sparse population and rugged slopes offered no great attraction either to trader or planter, and its early importance as a port diminished. The seaport of Apia, in Western Samoa, was then the center of activity, a metropolis of the Southern Ocean. It was not until 1900 when the United States assumed control over the eastern portion of the group and developed its naval station in Pago Pago harbor that Tutuila regained somewhat its early prestige. The Manua Islands, approachable only in small boats by precarious passage through reefs which are passable, only in fine weather, have tended to retain their historic isolation; together with the western end of Savaii, they form strongholds of traditional society.[5]

There is no surviving account of the voyages which brought the Polynesians to Samoa. Any attempt to reconstruct the story of the Western Pacific peoples up to their present widely scattered homelands leads to much disputed theories of their geographic origin. The possibility exists that the Polynesians arrived sometime in the 5th century. Those families occupying the Samoan archipelago, however, achieved a degree of unity and evolved a unique culture.[6]

It is generally conceded that the Samoan Islands were discovered by the Western world by Jacob Roggeveen, the Dutch explorer of the Pacific, on 13 June 1722. Louis de Bougainville visited them in 1768. The Frenchman LaPerouse lost some men at Tutuila in 1787 in an area now referred to as Massacre Bay.[7] Other notable explorers included the German Kotzebue, the English Captain Edwards of the *Pandora* in search of the *Bounty* mutineers, and French Captain Freycinet. Freycinet discovered Rose Island and named it after his wife.

By 1820 American traders had established commercial relations with the Samoan Islands but the initial American Naval experience was hardly a friendly one. Charles Wilkes, who had visited and described many islands earlier with the U.S. Exploring Expedition, made some trade agreements with the native chiefs during his explorations of these islands in 1839.[8] Shortly after this an American seaman with Wilkes was murdered on one of the islands and men from two of Wilkes' ships which were in the vicinity attempted in vain to obtain redress from the native ruler. They resorted to forming a landing party of sailors and marines supported by a preliminary bombardment from the ship which caused the natives to flee as they went ashore.[9] It is not difficult to understand the mistrust this incident engendered.

By the mid-1800s Germany, Great Britain, and the United States each had a stake in Samoa, which they proved tenacious in maintaining. The three powers became entangled in Samoan affairs and created a situation which was resolved by a fateful Act of God. Originating in a missionary interest, the British stake was more firmly entrenched by some trade, particularly throughout Sydney and Auckland. They also increased their influence by acquiring land. These factors combined with the increase of communication between the southwest Pacific and Canada, provided a fuller realization of the relative importance of Samoa.[10] More than once a British consul had suggested that the island group should be a British protectorate, but the British government declined to go beyond occasional naval intervention.

For the Americans, the Samoan involvement was an extension of their north Pacific trade centered in Hawaii, and it was vaguely connected to her interests in Panama and the projected canal. With the canal, Samoa became a major communications center of the Pacific, not the least because of the superb harbor of Pago Pago in Tutuila.

The German government considered the city of Apia to be the center of her influence in the Pacific and stationed a consul there. In April 1877 the German consular and naval authorities negotiated with native legislative authorities to achieve the two-part objective of establishing German interests in the islands and obtaining the recognition of Germany's equal rights in the event that treaties were concluded with other powers. The protocol signed on 3 July 1877 stated that, in the event of a war to protect German property, the Samoans would not grant preferential privileges to other powers and that Samoa would not accept the protection of any other power.[11]

Some months later, on 17 January 1878, a Samoan treaty was concluded with the United States assuring "most-favoured-nation" treatment and allowing the establishment of a U.S. naval base. Pago Pago on the island of Tutuila, the best harbor in Samoa, was selected. Ownership of the harbor was actually transferred to the United States by a deed executed on the American steamer *Adams* on 5 August of the same year. In the treaty, the United States agreed to offer her good offices in case of any difference between Samoa and any other power. These agreements obviously infringed upon the German treaty. According to Germany's point of view here was the germ of a U.S. protectorate and the German consul demanded an explanation from the Samoan authorities. Not receiving this they seized the ports of Saluafata and Fulealili as security for the conclusion of another treaty which would give Germany "most-favoured-nation" treatment in view of the American agreement. Such a treaty was eventually exacted from Samoa on 24 January 1879. With the grant of a naval and coaling station was coupled the promise not to give to any other nation such rights as had been given to Germany.

This document created so much uneasiness among the British residents of the islands that the High Commissioner for the Western Pacific proceeded to Samoa at the first opportunity to conclude an agreement with parallel privileges for British subjects. This treaty was signed on 28 August 1879. By Article VIII, Great Britain was granted the privilege, if she thought fit, of establishing a naval station and coaling depot in a Samoan harbor, provided it should not be in either of the harbors selected by the other two powers.

This potentially explosive situation built up from 1884 to 1889 and was resolved in an unexpected way—the catastrophic hurricane at Apia. Essentially all of the armadas of the jealous rival powers—very considerable armadas for the business in hand—was within a few hours strewn on the beach.

In the Samoan hurricane, The U.S. ships *Trenton* and *Vandalia* were totally wrecked in Apia and the *Nipsic* was saved only by being run aground in a cove. The British ship, *Calliope*, because of her greater steam power barely escaped to the sea and was roundly cheered as she crept through the doomed American ships unable to follow. Three German ships, the *Eber*, *Adler* and the *Olga*, were also wrecked. When day broke, a few score German and American seamen, unarmed and helpless, were all that remained of the crew of six warships. The good-natured Samoans, forgetting their factions and their injuries, pulled the exhausted sufferers from the surf and nursed them back to life.[12] Thus, the work of conciliation already begun in the chancellories in Europe was launched upon its course.[13]

The hurricane settled a critical international situation which had seemed to be on the verge of a serious break.[14] Three American warships, whose "old fashion engines and defective steampower" prevented their reaching the open sea where they could ride out the storm, were put out of commission. The loss served as tragic proof of the need for modern ships and left the United States with virtually no warships worthy of the name in the Pacific.[15]

In 1889 the Secretary of the Navy openly sought the acquisition of bases from which to service the new Atlantic and Pacific Fleets that he had proposed. Referring specifically to the Samoan Islands, he observed that the "necessity of establishing foreign coaling stations and the commercial importance of the islands, render it desirable to place this station (Samoa) as soon as possible on a permanent basis."[16] In addition, the Secretary pushed for the construction of three new warships with improved and more powerful engines. As a by-product of the hurricane, the permanency of U.S. use of Pago Pago harbor and an improvement in the capability of the fleet were achieved. Although the Navy Department had deposited a shipment of coal at Pago Pago to implement its treaty rights in 1880, it did not formally establish a naval base there until 1889.[17]

The final act of the Berlin Conference which followed the catastrophic hurricane recognized Samoa as an independent and neutral state and the three powers agreed on Malietoa Laupepa as King. A Supreme Court was set up with a single judge to be named by the three powers if they could agree; if they could not he was to be named by the King of Norway and Sweden. Alienation of lands was carefully guarded against and a commission was established to decide upon existing claims.[18]

Further fighting among the native factions occurred following the death of Malietoa Laupepa in 1898, an uprising requiring intervention once again by the respective powers supporting the native leader. The Convention of 1899 accepted the view that no solution could be found in tripartite government. Britain, therefore, in return for concessions in West Africa and the Solomon Islands, renounced in favor of Germany all her rights in the islands of Upolu and Savaii, and in favor of the United States, all in Tutuila and the islands east of 171°W. The islands were divided between Germany and the United States according to that arrangement.

Owing to the overwhelming distraction of the Boer War in South Africa, the agreement passed with relatively little notice. New Zealand, however, was deeply offended and the Prime Minister of New Zealand, R. J. Seddon, made no secret of his chagrin. He regretted the loss of Samoa, not because of her economic value, but because of the formidable strategic value she would possess if controlled by a foreign power. He wrote to the Colonial Office on 16 April 1900 as follows:

> The colonies of Australasia feel keenly the placing in the Pacific—the central group of the Pacific—fortified position of foreign powers that may in the future be used as bases of attack on them and their commerce. The colonists believe that there must have been some grave diplomatic reason for such a step not disclosed in the official documents, and as the matter has been ended it is useless to comment on the reasons put forward in the dispatch.

He added that "the surrender of Samoa will in the future be a source of anxiety and entail expense on Great Britain and the colonies in preparing for and providing against eventualities."[19]

As Samoa passed out of the British influence in the Pacific, the Germans raised their flag at Apia and Western Samoa became a German colony. Dr. Solf, who at the time was president of the municipality of Apia, was appointed governor. One analysis of the power play-off was offered by Lord Shaftesbury whc indicated in the House of Lords that the islands which England gave to Germany had no strategic value or importance to Great Britain.

They were important for another reason, however. They were the home (Hawaiki) of the Polynesian race most allied to the Maori. Thus, when the war broke out, Samoa was to New Zealand what New Guinea was to Australia—an irredenta in which honor was involved and which they hastened to redeem.[20]

On 29 August 1914 Dr. Schultz, who had taken over upon Dr. Solf's retirement, surrendered the Samoan islands to New Zealand troops who arrived under escort of the Australian naval squadron. The military occupation continued until 30 April 1920. By the Treaty of Versailles, the mandate for the future government of Western Samoa was offered to, and accepted by, New Zealand.[21]

The first ten years of New Zealand's administration of Western Samoa provided a record of endless political trouble and it appeared at one time as if the Southern Dominion would have to abandon the mandate. Whereas the Germans had ruthlessly suppressed political agitators and disturbances that occurred among the natives, the New Zealanders were more tolerant and accordingly they fell heir to political quarrels of which they knew little, and to native temper, sometimes morose, sometimes excitable, but nearly always hostile—all of which they made no effort to understand. The Samoans, an intelligent, proud, and capable people, actively resented the fact that their country had been handed over to New Zealand as a "C Class Mandate," that is, a mandate of primitive people incapable of governing themselves.[22]

The setting-up of the New Zealand administration prompted the formation of *Mau*, a nationalistic organization, stern of purpose and bitterly partisan, whose objectives ranged all the way from a demand for participation in local government to an agitation to make "Samoa for Samoans." Some of their demands were warranted in light of the fact that New Zealand had sent a few administrators whose only qualification was that they had distinguished themselves as officers in the 1914–1918 war. These military officers had no understanding of the Samoans' national feeling; to them the Samoans were simply a lot of stupid natives led by agitators who were trying to undermine established authority.[23]

The story of Western Samoa's development under New Zealand's administration since World War I outlined in a few phases: an exuberant burst of reforming energy in the first five or six years of the mandate; New Zealand's failure to help prepare the Samoans with the rapid pace of innovation; the Samoan reaction which, expressed in the *Mau* campaign of passive disobedience, caused the administration's progressive schemes to collapse; the disastrous riot of 1929 which gave the New Zealand rule a blow that undermined its confidence for 20 years; the depression and the long period of passivity in administration; improvement in the atmosphere beginning in 1935 and the development of new policies in the late 1940s; stimulation of activity provided by the able and imaginative administrator, Guy Powles.[24]

In 1946 a trusteeship agreement for Western Samoa replacing the former mandate was provided by the General Assembly of the United Nations. New Zealand, as the administering authority, formally pledged to promote the development of the territory toward self-government. The watershed in Western Samoan political development was the year 1947. Decisions were made that year which were intended to ensure that changes would be made as a result of free and amicable discussions and agreements and that New Zealand would help the Samoan leaders and people to gain experience to prepare themselves for each step towards self-government.[25] New Zealand hoped for the development of responsible government by stages, and for a gradual modification of the native Samoan institutions to meet the demands of the modern world.

A Constitutional Convention held in November–December 1954 showed that although Samoans were willing to develop the British form of parliamentary government, they desired to maintain some of their traditional customs in working it out. Because of the successful training period begun in 1947, self-government by the Samoans was introduced in 1959. A plebiscite on independence was held on 9 May 1961 and the United Nations consented to terminate the trusteeship in October 1961. The Independent State of Western Samoa came into existence on 1 January 1962, the first fully independent Polynesian state in the 20th century.

Western Samoa is now governed under a novel constitution closely related to the Samoan social system. The *matai*, or head of the extended family group, who has been the most important man in Samoan tribal life, continues to be the key figure in political life. Politics is largely conducted through the *matais*, who dominate the voting system. Objections to this arrangement in a society with democratic ambitions have been met with the argument that it suits the wishes of the Samoans, who are accustomed to express their views through their *matais*. This system was overwhelmingly endorsed by vote in a national plebiscite. The office of head of state is held jointly by two chiefs of leading families who have been outstanding in the history of the archipelago since it was first discovered, Tamasese and Malietoa.

For financial reasons Western Samoa has not sought membership in the United Nations nor has she joined the British Commonwealth, although she has joined the Economic Council for Asia and the Far East and the World Health Organization. At the present time diplomatic affairs are being handled through New Zealand embassies. Although not a United Nations member, she is benefiting from a U.N. program to raise standards throughout the South Pacific. Western Samoa received the initial emphasis from this program because it was the only independent nation served by the newly established United Nations Regional Office for the Western Pacific based in Apia. The United Nations' effort will focus on Western Samoa's foremost problem, slack agricultural production, with an eye toward what is expected to be its foremost future problem—expansion of population. Population is expected to rise from 114,000 in 1961 to 300,000 within 20 years.[26]

There are signs of change on the horizon. A generation is emerging that has less knowledge of, and hence tends to place less value on, some aspects of the old culture. It is anxious to acquire a greater knowledge of European institutions. All members of *aiga* (the extended family or relative) have a voice in the election of the *matai* and consequently an indirect voice in public affairs. Constantly improving educational facilities are making the people more aware of the part they can play in the development of the country. Most young men showing initiative and enterprise have good chances of becoming *matais*. Public meetings held in connection with the constitutional convention and the future government were well attended and discussions showed that many of the better-educated young people were actively interested in public affairs. This trend will likely continue and influence economic and political development in the future.

Western Samoa has performed as an oddly aloof and self-centered member of the free nations, but her aversion to the intrusion of the outside world is slowly giving way to reluctant acceptance. Most Western Samoans are poor. The inefficient, haphazard production of copra, bananas, cocoa, and coffee provides only subsistence livelihood for the majority and the annual per capita income of $60 is one of the lowest in the South Seas. After they became independent they did not want tourist or foreign investments. This attitude is changing as it becomes clear that both are needed to check poverty among the increasing population and to develop untapped agricultural and forest wealth.[27]

Western Samoan plans for development include construction of new hotels and related facilities and new airstrips to make travel easier to and from American Samoa, a regular stop on international airline routes. Western Samoa has been influenced by the more advanced economy of American Samoa to raise wages and this has increased the buying power of individuals. In addition to roads and housing, agriculture, forestry, fisheries with processing plants and harbors have been developed. An international staff made up of a score of experts under the direction of the United Nations representative for the Western Pacific Commission, is at work guiding the development program—one that seeks to maintain a balance between economic progress and the desires of the people to maintain their traditional ways.[28]

Some problems remain, however. Cash requirements are not excessive in this culture but needs are still greater than income. New food and export crops are urgently needed to cater to the growing population, but further land development is limited. Recommendations developing for secondary industries such as timber, coffee roasting, and fish canning have been made but securing the capital for the purpose remains to be a problem.[29] New Zealand, and Australia on a much smaller basis, both provide aid, but not enough to meet the need for capital.

In September 1966 the Western Samoan Prime Minister, Fiame Mataafa, reported that his quest for financial assistance to stimulate the economy had been a failure. Western Samoa had asked for one million dollars for dredging and improving the port of Asau on Savaii as part of a project to permit American Potlatch Forest, Incorporated, a wood product concern of San Francisco, to tap reserves on Savaii. The Secretary of State indicated that the United States could not help. The Prime Minister said:

> In view of the many millions it has spent in American Samoa, I do not see why Washington could not have helped us some too. I would not like to do it, but if I cannot get further aid from the free world, I am prepared to go to Moscow or Peking.[30]

The island groups of the Pacific are considerably interested in the political progress of Western Samoa. The trials and tribulations of the people as they move toward complete self-sufficiency are indicative of those yet to be faced in other archipelagoes. The lead and experience of Western Samoa are being closely followed by the people of Fiji, the Solomons, New Guinea, and the Cook Islands, and by those of French Polynesia and the island groups in Micronesia.

Following the period of political turbulence in which Western powers maneuvered for position in the South Pacific, American (then Eastern) Samoa was acquired by the United States in accordance with a convention by the United States, Great Britain, and Germany. This convention was signed 2 December 1899, ratified 16 February 1900, and proclaimed by the President of the United States on the latter date. By an Executive Order of 19 February 1900, the islands were placed under the authority of the Secretary of the Navy for use as a naval station. The high chiefs of Tutuila voluntarily ceded the islands of Tutuila and nearby Aunuu to the United States on 17 April 1900; the islands of the Manua group (Tau, Olosega and Ofu) were ceded by their chiefs on 16 July 1904. By joint resolution of Congress, approved 4 March 1925, Swain Island was annexed to American Samoa.[31]

In exercising jurisdiction over American Samoa and utilizing it as a naval base and coaling station, the Navy had the responsibility of providing an orderly government, promoting the welfare of the native population, and carrying out other obligations to the people and their land. Certain obstacles had to be overcome in dealing with a people whose life, language, culture and customs were far removed from anything in the background and experience of our naval administrators.

The Navy found itself saddled with governing a people whose unique social system was organized around a network of communal family groups, each giving allegiance to a chief, or *matai*, whose word was law. The *matai* determined the occupation of each member, apportioned earnings among the group and held in trust all family lands. Ascending echelons of the *matai* included numerous high chiefs and "talking" chiefs. No question could be decided save by prolix oratory and long dalliance around bowls of *kava*, Samoa's ceremonial drink. Impatient Navy post commandants and governors of American Samoa, whose tours of duty were brief, had neither time nor desire to reform such a society. Deciding that a "Samoa for Samoans" policy was best, the Navy for 51 years did little more than supply minimal education and health services.[32]

The government of American Samoa, as organized by the Navy, functioned directly under its jurisdiction for a number of years. From the start it was the Navy's general policy to encourage the people to be independent. It thus avoided Federal expenditures for other than purely naval affairs. Although this policy was eventually modified to the extent that Federal funds became available to supplement local resources in the establishment of certain public facilities and services, there was to all intent and purposes no government-sponsored education in American Samoa until 1921. Previously, education remained primarily with the missions. While the Navy made an early start in providing limited medical services and improving sanitation, it was not until April 1945 that work began on an urgently needed new hospital. This facility was completed and opened for service in March 1946. A start was made in 1900 to establish a public road around the Pago Pago Bay area. The Samoans had no experience or tools but willingly provided the labor. Little progress was made, however, until World War II. By 1951 there were only 3.5 miles of paved road, 38 miles of unpaved road, 28 miles of secondary roads and 50 miles of trails. Most of the system was on the island of Tutuila.

In World War II the islands became a staging area for Guadalcanal. Soon everybody was working for the military. Schools closed down, copra cutting ceased, hundreds of young Samoans deserted their traditional ways. Military expenditures brought a rush of prosperity and kept the *matai* busy dividing up the wages paid Samoan civilians. Samoa's position as a front line station in the war lasted only a few months, however, with no scars of war. Because of its location and its unsurpassed harbor, it was heavily fortified and even now, thirty years later, concrete pillboxes still ring the island, but only one shot was ever fired at it. A Japanese submarine surfaced north of Tutuila and lobbed a shell across the mountain in the general direction of Pago Pago. Ironically, it struck the home of a Japanese trader.

The United States Department of the Interior, responsible for Indian affairs and territories, had long been interested in American Samoa. In 1901 and again in 1911 the Navy asked its advice about raising the quality of education in the islands. In 1907 the President directed the Secretary of the Navy to send copies of all official correspondence regarding Samoa to the Department of the Interior. The Interior Department became actively interested in supplanting the Navy in Samoa and the other islands after World War II. A campaign directed toward that end by Secretary of the Interior Harold L. Ickes created a great deal of inter-departmental animosity, but on 18 June 1947 the Secretaries of State, War, Navy and Interior jointly recommended to the President that responsibility for American Samoa should be vested in the Department of the Interior. On 14 May 1949 the President directed the Secretaries of the Navy and the Interior to arrange for the transfer, and they agreed upon 1 July 1951 as the date for the changeover.[33]

Under naval control the Samoans had been governed by a benevolent paternalism. Their material wants were taken care of within the limits of naval resources and their wishes were respected so far as they were consistent with the smooth and efficient running of the station. Nevertheless, the Samoans were always incidental rather than central to the main concern of the government. This situation had its advantages: Samoan society was protected from some of the destructive effects of European contact which elsewhere in the Pacific produced a breakdown of society, and Samoa retained her village-dwelling life style and the traditional system of authority.[34]

The departure of the Navy, which had been spending many millions of dollars a year on its installation, payroll and services, left the island economy stripped. The governors appointed by the Department of the Interior, handicapped by an extremely small budget, came and went with alarming rapidity. (In one two-year period, the island had four governors and four acting governors.) Despite heroic efforts by a few of the more durable governors, conditions were scarcely better after ten years of the Interior's rule.

Federal grants and appropriations for the regular operations of American Samoa averaged less than $67 per capita a year from 1956 to 1960. Today, however, American Samoa is a showplace of the Pacific. Young expatriates are flooding back to participate in the islands' bursting new life and prosperity. Other islanders come to stare enviously at American Samoa's new schools and roads. Educators come to observe Samoa's exciting experiment, the first anywhere, in teaching almost totally by television. Its storied capital, Pago Pago, is now a main stop on the direct route from Hawaii to Australia. Tourists by the hundreds find Oceania's finest airport, a new luxury hotel and an idyllic South Sea setting.[35]

What brought about this metamorphosis? Two factors are mainly responsible: the threat of a diplomatic disaster and a dynamic man. Early in 1961, the U.S. realized that in July of the next year American Samoa was slated as host for the triennial meeting of the South Pacific Conference. More than 200 delegates would be coming from other Pacific territories. Worldwide radio and press coverage would contrast America's vaunted concern for the world's underprivileged with the shabby neglect of her own.

Appalled at this prospect, President Kennedy rushed to Congress a request for an emergency appropriation of $465,000. He instructed the Department of the Interior to appoint a new governor to handle the project swiftly. Secretary Stewart Udall picked a seasoned troubleshooter, H. Rex Lee, 52, then Deputy Commissioner of the Bureau of Indian Affairs—a man of steely determination masked by a soft-spoken manner. His assignment to American Samoa was the same as Sir Guy Powles' previous assignment had been to Western Samoa in the stimulation of the vitality and prosperity of the area.

After he had been in office only a month he returned to Washington where he explained to members of the House Subcommittee on Deficiency Appropriations: "When the islands were necessary for our defense, up to and including World War II, we used them and their people." Expanding on the territory's importance, he remarked:

> Here is our chance to show the world how we can help undeveloped peoples toward a self-sufficient life. These people in Samoa are so nice they just haven't been heard in the world of gimme-gimme. Help and attention seem to go where the screaming is. American dereliction has resulted in a faulty education, inadequate roads, bad communications, and a lack of preparation for self-government and economic competition.[36]

The result was congressional approval of $5 million on the $9.5 million requested for the first year (1962) with consideration given for the $12 million needed for 1963. With Samoa "getting along" on annual appropriations of $2 million, this windfall provided for expansion of education, including construction of five junior high schools, two senior high schools, as well as a start on the third senior high school. Construction progressed on the airfield at Tufuna and on an attractive auditorium for the South Pacific Conference meeting, which later could be used for school and public functions.[37]

Back in Samoa, Governor Lee was everywhere at once checking, prodding and approving, and Pago Pago's appearance changed markedly. The waterfront was swept clear of over-the-water latrines. Villages were cleaned up and flowers were planted. Seabees "on loan" from a personal friend, Rear Admiral Henry G. Clark of the 14th Naval District in Hawaii, supervised road building and gave the Samoans on-the-job training. Some 5,500 gallons of paint was flown in, sold at cost, and Samoans painted virtually everything. By the time the South Pacific Conference delegates arrived the Samoans could proudly display: a jet airport complete with its 9,000 foot runway, 15 miles of 20-foot wide macadam roads leading to the beauty spots of Tutuila, 29 new teachers, housing units with modern plumbing, 3 new buildings for Samoa's high school capable of accomodating 300 visitors during the conference; the handsome new civic auditorium, and a new power plant; and 20,000 immensely proud Samoans.

When Governor Lee mapped out his grand strategy in 1961 for Samoan redemption, he indicated: "Simply to fix this place up for the South Pacific Conference (SPC) meeting and then abandon it would be worse than nothing."[38] With this as a theme, continued effort has been directed toward the improvement and self-sufficiency of American Samoans. Pago Pago Intercontinental, a 100-room, air-conditioned hotel is as modern as its Western counterparts. Its stockholders are some 1,200 islanders, each of whom must be 51 percent Samoan to buy shares. The Samoan equity has been supplemented by loans from the United States Area Redevelopment Administration and the Bank of Hawaii. The hotel is operated by a wholly owned subsidiary of Pan American Airways, which serves the territory by jet aircraft.

The old educational system has been replaced by a revolutionary program. Governor Lee reasoned that Samoan education could not rely on conventional, institutional means, but that educational TV might be the answer. With a small congressional appropriation for a feasibility study, Lee brought to Samoa a four-man study group from the National Association of Educational Broadcasters. After several years of considerable planning and activity, educational television was launched in Samoa. Today television is in many classrooms and is one of the chief medium of instruction. To service the new program, the government has built a new, six-channel television station, the finest in the South Pacific, and elaborate facilities for preparing and broadcasting lessons. Twenty-two elementary schools and three high schools have been constructed.

Per capita income has doubled during the last decade. No longer is there widespread unemployment. Jobs are even held by several thousand immigrants from the neighboring state of Western Samoa. Clearly American Samoa is prospering and emerging as the showcase of the South Pacific. The development programs are to go on for several years with annual expenditures of more than twice the old budgets. More and more often the projects are being financed by raising local revenues. The Samoans showed their gratitude by the legislature's action in early 1963 when it overwhelmingly voted "to join our fellow Americans in paying Federal income tax," and in doing so Samoa became the only American territory voluntarily to take on this burden. One Samoan legislator who spoke against the tax as "colonialistic" and "undemocratic" was cried down by a whole Phalanx of fellow chiefs. High Chief Rapi Sotoa, President of the Senate, said, "We have never been less colonialist or more democratic. This makes us real Americans at last."[39]

American Samoa seems well on the road to development planned by the government. One question that the future holds is whether they will develop the skills and self-reliance to continue on their own. The hope is that their lush tropical island with Tutuila's beautiful hill-girt harbor as the main attraction will eventually become a major resort. Tourist trade offers the best prospect to Samoa for attaining a self-sustaining income since the territory lacks abundant natural resources.[40]

Since the Samoan Islands were divided in 1899, there has been speculation on the possibility of their being reunited. Today there seems to be less likelihood than ever before. American Samoa has become strongly attached to the United States and the Western Samoans show little inclination to attempt to incorporate their eastern cousins. The two Samoas are becoming more and more distant for several reasons. One is the fact that Washington rushed efforts to make up for a decade of neglect in American Samoa and in doing so put the Eastern Samoans economically ahead of their western cousins. Partly because of this American Samoa is experiencing social change at a faster rate than Western Samoa. The disparity between the two economically is shown in the difference in income. The per capita income is higher than $400 for the 26,000 people of American Samoa while it is about $60 for the 135,000 people of Western Samoa.

There are extensive family connections between the people of the two Samoas, and there will always be close contact between the two. However, there is now a larger number of American Samoans in the United States as a result of migration over the years than in American Samoa itself. Families are now tied closer to the "mainland," as the United States is called, than to Western Samoa.

The people find it more or less acceptable to be a part of the United States. A constitutional convention provides for discussions about increasing the scope of representative government. United States officials foresee some eventual change from the present status of an unincorporated territory of the United States, a status that gives American Samoans U.S.

nationality but not full citizenship. They can go freely to the United States and become citizens, but as nationals they do not have the right to vote and do not have the obligation to serve in the military.[41]

In 1964 the United Nations Special Committee on Colonialism decided by a vote that the United States was lagging in its work toward independence for the people of American Samoa. The committee indicated that, while progress had been made, American Samoa was still far from self-government and independence.[42]

The Samoan legislature flew into an uproar when word reached Samoa of this statement and that a Communist representative had risen in the United Nations to call American Samoa "a familiar example of colonialist conquest." "Let us make it plain," said one spokesman, "that American Samoa is no colony but a part of the United States—*by choice*. And let no one come calling here to force us apart from our brothers, the mainland Americans."[43]

4 / New Guinea

John L. Butts,

Captain, United States Navy

Due north of Australia, near the eastern end of the island chain which ties the Australian continent to Asia, lies New Guinea—the second largest island in the world. Discovered by the Portuguese and claimed by Spain, portions of New Guinea and the surrounding islands have at various times been annexed by Britain, Germany, and the Netherlands; invaded by Australians, Japanese, and Indonesians; mandated by the League of Nations; and placed under United Nations Trusteeship. For a brief period in 1962–63 West New Guinea was under the direct administration of the United Nations and therefore claims the distinction of being the first territory ever to be governed by an international organization.

The island is covered in most areas by some of the densest jungle in the world and it is inhabited largely by people only now emerging from the Stone Age. Down its middle lies a great range of mountains, with peaks so high that during World War II the New Guinea cordillera was known as the "Little Hump" by aviators who flew over it.

New Guinea was strategically important in both world wars and is of continuing international interest today. West New Guinea, or West Irian, is now under the control of Indonesia, while the eastern portion of the island is administered by Australia. The northeastern sector, together with the islands of the Bismarck Archipelago and the islands of Buka and Bougainville in the Solomons, form the Trust Territory of New Guinea which Australia holds under trusteeship from the United Nations. The southeastern sector and several adjacent groups of small islands comprise the colony of Papua. Australia administers these areas together as the Territory of Papua-New Guinea.

Though sovereignty over West New Guinea has passed from the Netherlands to Indonesia, and though Australia now administers the sector of the island which was once the German colony of Kaiser Wilhelmsland, (now North-East New Guinea) the boundaries of New Guinea's three principal divisions have changed but little since the island was partitioned in 1884. In that year demands from Australian colonists for unclaimed portions of New Guinea and moves by Chancellor Bismarck to acquire a colonial empire for Germany led Britain and Germany to divide between them that part of New Guinea not claimed by the Dutch. Both the British and the Germans accepted the 141st meridian as the boundary of Dutch New Guinea apparently respecting Dutch assertions based upon right of discovery, occupation and suzerainty over native leaders who controlled an area of which western New Guinea was a part.

Active Australian interest in annexing New Guinea was evident at least as early as 1867. In 1882 the Premier of Queensland, Sir Thomas McIlwraith, fearing that Germany intended to establish a colony in New Guinea—and convinced that Britain would take no action to claim any part of the island, took matters in his own hands and claimed eastern New Guinea for Queensland. The British Government disavowed McIlwraith's unilateral action but did negotiate the issue with the Australian colonists and agreed ultimately to appoint a High Commissioner for New Guinea. British ships met at Port Moresby and a protectorate over the southeastern part of the island was proclaimed in November and December 1884. The proclamation by the commander of the naval squadron was actually the third such pronouncement in the name of Great Britain, McIlwraith's representative and the newly-appointed Deputy Commissioner for New Guinea having claimed the area also and raised the British flag on two earlier occasions. The three separate flag raisings have been described as the height of colonial comic opera.[1]

The authorities in Australia had urged that all of Papua not claimed by the Dutch be annexed as a barrier to further non-British encroachment in the area. The desire for annexation of a broad area was widespread in Australia at the time and was a direct reflection of Australian concern about German expansion. The proclamation, however, did not accommodate this desire. The northeastern territory was excluded.[2]

The decision to proclaim a protectorate over only the southeastern portion of New Guinea was a deliberate choice of the British Government—

an attempt to reach accord with Germany during a trying period. Lord Granville's official statement to the German Ambassador was that "the extension of some form of British authority in New Guinea . . . will only embrace that part of the island which specially interests the Australian Colonies, without any prejudice to any territorial questions beyond those limits."[3] Paul W. van der Veur, the journalist observes that "if this statement was not intended as a signal to go ahead, the Germans may be pardoned for interpreting it as such." Since the Australians wanted all of New Guinea to the east of the area claimed by the Dutch, London's decision to limit its claim was made at some expense to the interests of the colonists. At least the Australians believed the Imperial government had ceded the territory rightfully claimed by Australia. It is interesting to note that thirty-five years later in the peace settlement of the World War, the British Government was still at odds with the demands of Australian opinion; this time in an effort to reach accord with the President of the United States.

The Germans, acting upon the latitude afforded by the language of the British proclamation, raised the German flag over the northeastern part of New Guinea and nearby islands. In contrast to their extremely repressive policies in Africa, the Germans in New Guinea "found time to build roads and bridges, lay out townships and establish plantations which are a lasting tribute to the German colonist."[4] German efforts in this regard are all the more noticeable because neither Australia nor the Netherlands attempted to do much with their sectors of New Guinea during that period. The Australians, however, remained concerned about occupation of the island areas on her northern doorstep by the Germans.

The First World War brought an end to Australia's fear of the German menace. Although the outbreak of the war apparently came as somewhat of a surprise to most Australians, the armed forces were quickly mobilized. "At the request of the British Government and on the clear understanding that Australia was to act merely as an agent, the Australian Government in 1914 secured by force the German colonies to the north of Australia."[5] W. J. Hudson, the author, states emphatically that "the initiative was Britain's and Britain reserved the right to negotiate the subsequent disposal of the colonies. . . ." But, Guy H. Scholefield maintains that "it was on behalf of the Allies collectively that Australia seized Kaiser Wilhelm's land and Bismarck."[6]

Having gained control of an area they had wanted to annex only thirty years earlier, the Australians were understandably reluctant to give it up. They believed that Australia should control all of New Guinea not held by the Dutch and the Bismarck Archipelago as well. To the Australians, the group of islands was—an area whose control by a foreign power would be to Australia's disadvantage—strategically important.

Australia's perception as to the worth of New Guinea differed substantially from views held by the British Government. To Australia, control of New Guinea was a matter of the highest importance. To Britain, Dominion retention of captured colonies was supported in principle, but it was a principle to which the British Government was far less than committed.

Unfortunately, Australia's assumption that she would fall heir automatically to the German colony she had captured ran contrary to President Wilson's idea of her role, that is his call for the people of all colonies to have a voice on questions of sovereignty which would be given "equal weight with the equitable claims of the government whose title is to be determined."[7] The result was the famous conflict between the Australian Prime Minister, William Morris Hughes, and President Wilson at the Paris Peace Conference. In the face of formidable opposition, Hughes was cast in the role of defender of Australian nationalism, and of the long-standing "White Australia" policy. This much-debated policy, begun in the aftermath of the Australian gold rush to prevent an influx of Chinese labor, was later broadened to such a point that only Anglo-Saxons could be assured of entry approval.

Above all else, Hughes sought control of the former German colonies south of the equator. His objective was security for Australia—freedom from the threat of immigration and "deliverance from the possibility of nearby fortification by a potentially unfriendly power." Mr. Hughes remained very much concerned with the question of Australian security for many years after the war.

Leadership out of the impending impasse was provided by Prime Minister Botha of the Union of South Africa. He said that he would be prepared to accept the idea of a mandate system—a concept which had been advanced by General J. C. Smuts of South Africa as a practical suggestion for disposing of the former Turkish territories by the League of Nations holding them as a "sacred trust of civilization." President Wilson had broadened Smuts's proposal to encompass all of Germany's colonies as well, a move which was poorly received by Australia and South Africa. The final refinement to the idea was suggested by David Lloyd George: the mandates would be given a classification based upon their supposed stage of development. It was this last proposal which Prime Minister Botha said he would accept and with which Mr. Hughes reluctantly agreed.[8]

Article 22 of the Covenant of the League of Nations provides for the mandated territories. With respect to the German colonies in the Pacific, the article states in part: "There are territories, such as South West Africa and certain of the Pacific Islands, which . . . can be best administered under the laws of the mandatory as integral portions of its territory. . . ." In December 1920 Australia was appointed the mandatory for the Territory of New Guinea by the Council of the League of Nations acting upon the decision of the Supreme Council of May 1919.

The mandates system has been described as a "new and enlightened approach to colonialism and . . . a practical expedient for sharing the spoils of war among the victors without too great a violation of non-annexation pledges"[9]—a compromise between the desires of the Commonwealth Prime Ministers for annexation of the conquered territories and the idealism of Wilson's Fourteen Points. Certainly the system as it ultimately evolved placed the mandatory in a position of almost total control, with little provision for the degree of control by the League for which General Smuts had called.

In light of Prime Minister Hughes's avowed intent to retain control of the former German colony adjacent to Australia, acceptance of the mandate by the Australian Government seems to be proof that the system was viewed as annexation in another guise, or at the least as a measure of control sufficient to protect Australia—in its own views—from the threat of immigration and foreign encroachment. Having attained the control which they sought over the people of the New Guinea area, "Australian governments over the next two decades were inclined to pay a minimum of further attention to them."[10]

In the years between the wars neither the Dutch nor the Australians made any notable progress in their respective sectors of New Guinea. The Dutch still considered West New Guinea an unhealthy backwater but were benevolently paternalistic for the most part toward the Papuans; the Australians were offered little economic incentive to develop the territory. The result was little progress, although to Australia's credit was her continuous consideration for the interests of the inhabitants of New Guinea.

Exploration was slow. Years went by and still there were many areas still marked "unknown territory" on the map. However, while Dutch New

Guinea remained almost a closed sector, Papua-New Guinea attracted a stream of adventurers and was very much a pioneer area.

World War II brought a sudden end to the placid pace of development in New Guinea. In Papua-New Guinea the flood of military equipment and personnel substantially changed the economic and social structures of the territory; and to the west, the war awoke the forces of Indonesian nationalism which would eventually wrest West New Guinea from the Dutch.

New Guinea and the Netherlands Indies were early items on Japan's agenda of conquest for the Pacific; they were the southern anchors of the island arc which the Japanese hoped to build around the Empire. Shortly after the attack on Pearl Harbor, the Netherlands Indies were overrun and in March 1942 Japan invaded New Guinea. Over the next two years, the battle for New Guinea became one of the hardest-fought campaigns of the war. Port Moresby, Milne Bay, Wau, Buka and Bougainville became household words in the United States and the Australians themselves became better acquainted with the island to their north. Although New Guinea's coasts had been recaptured from the Japanese by mid-1944, the New Guinea campaign did not end until May 1945. The price was high. Fifteen thousand Australian troops were killed or wounded in the fighting.

As the war drew to an end, the future of the underdeveloped regions of the world was discussed more frequently and debated in international conferences, and it became a major issue when the charter of the United Nations was drafted. Part of the debate was the result of heightened awareness, internationally, of the problem. Suddenly every major nation—and many minor ones as well—was an expert on colonial affairs, each with its own unassailable solution as how to best remedy the world's colonial ills. Another contingent demanded complete, and in many cases instant, independence for everyone.

One result of this interest and discussion was a considerably greater concern for colonial matters by the United Nations than by the League. The Covenant of the League of Nations covers dependent territories in a single article (Article 22). The United Nations Charter devotes seventeen articles—three entire chapters—exclusively to such territories, and the entire charter reflects U.N. interest in, and concern for, dependent peoples.

In the charter, as ultimately approved, Chapter XII, Article 75, provides that: "The United Nations shall establish under its authority an international trusteeship system for the administration and supervision of such territories as may be placed thereunder by subsequent individual agreements."

On 13 December 1946 the International Trusteeship System was established by U.N. resolution. Among the territories placed under United Nations supervision was the formerly mandated territory of New Guinea to be administered by Australia. Although the language of the trusteeship agreement promised more than that of the mandate, the degree of international supervision for which it provided was little changed. Australia was—and is—still fully in control of the territory.[11] (All but one of the former mandates of the League of Nations were placed under U.N. supervision. The sole exception was South West Africa, which South Africa declined to place under trusteeship.)

Australia's other New Guinean territory—Papua—was also included in the charter of the United Nations. Building upon the language of the Atlantic Charter, the discussions at San Francisco in the formative days of the U.N. led to a *Declaration Regarding Non-Self-Governing Territories.* This declaration, which is set forth as Chapter XI of the U.N. Charter, states in part that: "Members of the United Nations which have or assume responsibilities for the administration of territories whose people have not yet attained a full measure of self-government . . . accept as a sacred trust the obligation to promote to the utmost . . . the well-being of the inhabitants of these territories. . . ." Among the territories enumerated as falling within this category was Papua. At its first session the General Assembly pointed out that the obligations envisioned under Chapter XI were independent of trusteeship agreements and could be acted upon without the requirement of a Trusteeship Council—the administering body of the trusteeship system—in being.

In all of these U.N. actions, Australia played a leading role. Despite long-standing interest in New Guinea—certainly justified by the war—the Australian Government voluntarily placed the territory under a system of control which could eventually result in its independence from Australian supervision. Further, Australia was a prime mover in the establishment of principles of operation for the trusteeship system as a whole.

The Dutch, however, were not so progressive in this regard as were the Australians. Although the Netherlands voluntarily listed the Netherlands Indies as one of the territories falling under the provisions of Chapter XI of the Charter they were somewhat forced by circumstances to do so. Indonesia had proclaimed its independence on 17 August 1945, and the Dutch were involved in a colonial war for the next four years. In West

New Guinea, however—only recently liberated from the Japanese—the proclaimed independence of Indonesia was a matter of little interest. In spite of the establishment of the Republic of Indonesia in 1949, the Dutch retained control of West New Guinea.

Thus, in the years immediately following the war, New Guinea and the adjacent areas underwent several changes in political alignment. The change in status of the Trust Territory of New Guinea from a League of Nations mandate to a trusteeship of the United Nations caused scarcely a ripple—at first—in the Australian political pond, nor did the inclusion of Papua and West New Guinea as territories scheduled for eventual self-determination under the provisions of Chapter XI of the Charter prove of any immediate consequence. The trusteeship system was still in a period of shakedown and consolidation, with many U.N. member nations still uncertain—or in disagreement—as to the objectives sought. With each passing year, however, the administrators of the U.N. trusteeship system became ever more confident and demanding in their relations with those nations signatory to trusteeship agreements. This was because of the increasing clamor for full self-determination of all still-dependent territories raised by the new member nations from Africa and Asia in the U.N.

Dwight D. Eisenhower, commenting on the "spirit of nationalism" which had grown in the aftermath of the war, said: "The determination of the people for self-rule, their own flag, and their own vote in the United Nations resembled a torrent overrunning everything in its path, including, frequently, the best interests of those concerned."[12]

New Guinea, among the last of the vestiges of colonial rule, was one of the areas in the path of the torrent. In 1960 seventeen Afro-Asian nations achieved independence and became members of the U.N. In that same year the pattern of United Nations activities with regard to "anti-colonial" matters changed markedly.

One of the first steps taken by the new voting bloc was a *Declaration on the Granting of Independence to Colonial Countries and Peoples*. This declaration, passed by the General Assembly as Resolution 1514 (XV) of 14 December 1960, sets forth this basic premise:

> Immediate steps shall be taken, in Trust and Non-Self-Governing Territories or all other territories which have not yet attained independence, to transfer all powers to the people of these territories, without any conditions or reservations, in accordance with their freely expressed will and desire, without any distinction as to race, creed or color, in order to enable them to enjoy complete independence and freedom.

The language of this declaration, in effect, called for the establishment of target dates for independence for all still-dependent territories, a procedure which ran hard against the policy of the Australian government of going slowly in the matter of granting independence to Papua-New Guinea. Australia's reasons for this approach were explained by Mr. Paul Hasluck, Minister for Territories, in a 1960 statement to the House of Representatives in Canberra:

> Except where modifications have been made as a result of the coming of Europeans, New Guinea is still almost unbelievably primitive. . . . There is nothing yet even faintly resembling a sense of nationalism or a sense of community over the whole territory. . . . At this present time, the world would be acting in ignorance if it did not appreciate the primitive and unique character of the conditions in the territory and the size of the basic civilizing tasks to be completed. The administering power and the advanced native peoples with whom it is working need time for the job.[13]

There was another factor which, for a time, was even more of a political complication for the future of New Guinea than the demands of the new nations in the U.N.—the growing pains of Australia's neighbor, the Republic of Indonesia, which achieved its independence in 1949. From 1945 to 1960 Australian policy changed with successive Australian governments from support of the Dutch to support of Indonesia's national aspirations. This policy, based largely upon domestic considerations, was Australia's own—as was her stand on West New Guinea—and not a reflection of the interests of other nations.

Insofar as West New Guinea was concerned, Australia feared that Indonesia's claims to the area might—in the heat of nationalist fervor—be broadened to encompass eastern New Guinea. These fears were reduced to what has been described as a "nagging friction" after Sukarno made it clear in a press conference that Indonesia did not want eastern New Guinea.

Yet, the political future of the two areas remained far from decided, despite intensive international efforts in the U.N. and elsewhere to resolve the issue of West New Guinea. In Indonesia, the demand for West New Guinea—called West Irian grew in intensity. Indonesia claimed that West New Guinea "rightfully belonged to her and should be freed from Dutch colonial rule. The Netherlands maintained that the Papuans of West New Guinea were not Indonesians and therefore should be allowed to decide their own future when they were ready to do so."[14]

After the dispute had progressed to the point of limited Dutch-Indo-nesian military engagements—with the Indonesians getting the worst of it —a settlement was negotiated by the United Nations. On 15 August 1962 the Netherlands and Indonesia signed an agreement under the terms of which the Netherlands agreed to turn over West New Guinea to the United Nations, which in turn later would "have discretion to transfer all or parts of the administration to Indonesia."[15] By any standard, this agreement was a face-saving device, a measure to permit the Netherlands to bow to the international will rather than Indonesian threats and to allow Indonesia to attain her immediate objectives without disastrous con-sequences. Although it has been alternately praised and damned, the agreement is nonetheless an interesting example of successful U.N. peace-keeping and was probably the best available settlement of the issue, under the circumstances, which could have been obtained at the time. The terms of the Agreement of 15 August 1962 between the Governments of Indo-nesia and the Netherlands called for the administration of West New Guinea to be transferred to the United Nations Temporary Executive Authority. The United Nations established this Authority to administer the territory by resolution of the General Assembly on the effective date of the Dutch-Indonesian Agreement, the first time that any international organization had been so charged; but it was to be a brief tenure. Under pressure from Indonesia, the U.N. agreed to transfer full control to Indo-nesia, and on 1 May 1963 the changeover in government was accomplished. The U.N.'s compliance with Indonesian demands led to comments from some quarters that it was obviously permissable to be a colonial power if you were a member of the Afro-Asian Bloc.

In the meanwhile, on the Australian side of the border, United Nations influence was also making itself felt. Demands from the Trusteeship Coun-cil in the United Nations—and from various other members of the U.N.'s Fourth Committee as well—for early independence for Papua-New Guinea were reflected in a statement made by the Australian Prime Minister Menzies, upon his return to Australia from a trip abroad in June 1960. Mr. Menzies said:

> Whereas at one time many of us might have thought that it was better to go slowly in granting independence so that all conditions existed for a wise exercise of self-government, I think the prevailing school of thought today is that if in doubt you should go sooner not later. I belong to that school of thought myself, now, though I didn't once.[16]

To many analysts who had been following Australia's actions regarding New Guinea, this was an extraordinary statement. At the least, it was contrary to the statement on New Guinea which the Minister for Territories, Paul Hasluck, had made only a few days earlier. At the most, "it could be interpreted as an initial response to the request of the Trusteeship Council of the United Nations that Australia set target dates for the development of New Guinea toward self-government."[17] By any measure, Mr. Menzies had changed his mind and with it Australia's policy toward independence for New Guinea.

There were many factors which certainly must have influenced the decision to opt for self-government for New Guinea sooner rather than later —the changing international environment, Indonesian independence, Australia's changing perception of its strategic position, and reassessment of the potential of Papua-New Guinea. The most compelling factor, however, was almost certainly the ever increasing pressure from the U.N. for early self-determination for territories under trusteeship.

U.N. pressure notwithstanding, Australia has not yet been willing to go so far as to set a target date for full independence for New Guinea; but there is no question that Australia is, indeed, committed to ultimate independence for the territory. The long-held belief that, for strategic reasons, Australia must control New Guinea has apparently been overtaken by a more realistic appraisal of the island's strategic value in today's environment.

Australia has repeatedly reaffirmed her willingness to accept any changes in sovereignty or political affiliation of West New Guinea that are brought about through legal, peaceful measures. However, her unease about external influence in the course of political events in Indonesia—particularly the confrontation with Malaysia—was apparent in the months before the attempted coup in October 1965 by the Indonesian communists.[18] And in her own area, Australia is making a strong effort to prepare the inhabitants to stand on their own. In 1960 four separate pieces of legislation were passed, giving New Guinea's inhabitants a firmer voice in their own behalf. In 1964 general elections were held and further political development has proceeded apace. There was, however, no hint of what might be called "national politics" in the 1964 elections. By the spring of 1971 steps toward self-government in New Guinea had so progressed that a committee of the Papua-New Guinea House of Assembly, the Committee on Constitutional Development, recommended in its final report that steps be taken to prepare the area to govern itself by 1976. This committee did not recommend, however, that 1976—or any firm date—be selected as a target date for self-government, on the grounds that the local populace did not yet want self-government. But the committee did make recommendations concerning the ultimate structure of the government, proposed that Papua-New Guinea be called Niu Gini (pidgin English spelling), and suggested a design for a national flag.

These are constructive steps. The problems yet to be overcome before independence for the territory can be meaningfully achieved are formidable. Witchcraft, superstition, the famed "cargo cults," the language barrier, the lack of economic viability and a host of other problems remain. Margaret Mead, who has probably studied the peoples of New Guinea more closely than anyone else, has expressed this view:

> . . . the problem of nation-building in the eastern half of the immense island of New Guinea does . . . present very complicated problems. In this area . . . live some 2,000,000 Melanesians and Papuans. . . . They have been cut off from the rest of the world for thousands of years and at the time of discovery lacked any knowledge of script, metals, the wheel, the plough or any form of political organization capable of uniting originally disparate people.[19]

In Papua-New Guinea the educational and economic problems alone are so overwhelming as to seem almost to defy solution. Yet, despite these problems, the United Nations continues to press Australia for a target date for independence.

Australian authorities are working diligently to this end; but in so backward an area it is difficult to hurry. Nonetheless, real progress is being made. Members of the House of Assembly, the legislative body of Australian New Guinea, are largely elected. The size and functions of this body were expanded in 1968 and it is becoming an increasingly effective unit as time passes.

On the Indonesian side of the border, educational and economic problems are as bad as, or worse, than those in the Australian territory. The political future of West New Guinea, though, apparently has been decided.

Under the terms of its 1962 Agreement with the Netherlands, Indonesia undertook to provide for "an act of free choice" by the people of West New Guinea before the end of 1969.[20] As the date for this event approached, some of the Papuan tribesmen became increasingly restive and an active separatist movement developed in West New Guinea. Indonesia accused Australia and the Netherlands of supporting, if not fomenting, the unrest. By early May 1969 the uprising had reached such proportions that Indonesia sent a military force reported as 500 paratroopers to restore order.

In August 1969 the "act of free choice" was provided. There was no plebiscite, however. Instead, Indonesian authorities arranged a consultation with tribal chiefs and urban residents said to represent the entire population. About 1000 such leaders were consulted. With their approval, and despite continuing, widespread, native opposition, Indonesia formally annexed the territory.

The United Nations appears to be content with the Indonesian action and the political future of West New Guinea as an integral part of the Republic of Indonesia. But for the Australian territory the questions remain: When can independence be granted, and in what form? Can Papua-New Guinea really become a viable political unit, or will a wider association—such as the entire island of New Guinea, the Bismarck Archipelago, and the northern Solomons—be required? Can any such political unit stand alone, or will some sort of affiliation with the Commonwealth, Australia, Indonesia or some other nation be required? And just what sort of political future will Australia and Indonesia and the United Nations permit the area to pursue? [21]

Acceptable answers to these questions will not be easily arrived at, and the solutions which finally emerge may not be the ones now envisaged as most likely. Finally, the sought for objectives, whatever they may be, will probably not be achieved within the ambitious time schedule sought by the United Nations. For in a land with little knowledge of even the wheel, it is difficult to build a political machine.

Part II   Micronesia

5 / Micronesia and Self-Determination

Dwight A. Lane,

Captain, United States Navy

With the end of the Second World War, the worldwide colonial system, as it had previously been known, fell apart. A strong sense of idealism pervaded the world. Not only those countries formerly under the colonial rule of the defeated powers, but also all other dependent peoples came under the scrutiny of world opinion and the newly created United Nations. From this moment onward, the former colonial powers were on the defensive. And, included with them, came the United States, which had never considered itself a colonial power. Caught in the cross-fire of anticolonialism, the more moderate countries such as Australia, New Zealand, and the United States found themselves aligned with the more staunch die-hard colonial powers like South Africa and Portugal. Their reasons for holding on to their possessions varied, but certainly one of them was the constant fear of being challenged about the administration of their own territories.[1]

In 1960 the United Nations finally came to grips with the problem of "colonialism" largely because of pressure by the Afro-Asian countries and the Soviet Union. The Soviets initially introduced a draft resolution demanding that "all colonial countries and Trust and Non-Self-Governing Territories must be granted forthwith complete independence and freedom" and all "strongholds of colonialism in the form of possessions and leased areas in the territory of other states must be eliminated." These were rather strong words for the times, and the resolution was defeated.[2] The United States, as the Administering Authority of the Pacific Trust Territory obviously could not approve such a resolution, for it would have brought even such areas as Guam, the Virgin Islands, and Puerto Rico under immediate and direct scrutiny.

Although the Soviet resolution had been defeated, there followed the precedence-shattering *Declaration on the Granting of Independence to Colonial Countries and Peoples,* the Magna Charta for anti-colonialism, which called on all colonial powers to take "immediate steps . . . to transfer all powers to the peoples" of colonial territories.[3] The United States representative, in explanation of his abstaining vote, stated that his country was in favor of the principles of the advancement of human freedom but could not vote for the resolution unless it could vote for every word in it, the questionable words, most likely, being "immediate . . . transfer of powers." He, no doubt, also found the clause declaring that "inadequacy of political, economic, social, or educational preparedness should never serve as a pretext for delays in independence" to be fraught with danger.

As the next year's session of the General Assembly was about to open, it became apparent that "colonialism" would once again be prominent on the agenda, and the Soviet Union was expected to be active in forcing strong measures into the Assembly. President Kennedy then took the opportunity to address the General Assembly on September 25, 1961, to explain the basic United States position on colonialism.

> My country intends to be a participant and not merely an observer, in the peaceful, expeditious movement of nations from the status of colonies to the partnership of equals. . . . But colonialism in its harshest forms is not only the exploitation of new nations by old, of dark skins by light—or the subjugation of the poor by the rich. . . . And that is why there is no ignoring the fact that the tide of self-determination has not yet reached the Communist empire. . . . Let us debate colonialism in full—and apply the principle of free choice and the practice of free plebescites in every corner of the globe.[4]

Thus, was the keynote set for the U.S. position in all subsequent debates where colonialism was involved.

President Kennedy's address was followed by a draft resolution introduced by the Soviet Union calling for the "unconditional liquidation" of colonialism not later than the end of 1962. The resolution was eventually withdrawn without being put to a vote when the Soviet delegation was unable to muster any appreciable support among the other delegations.[5]

The resolution which was finally passed by the Assembly (UNGA Resolution 1654 of November 1961) expressed its regret that the response to the call for "immediate steps" to transfer power to the peoples of the territories had been minimal and decided to establish a Special Committee.[6] During the next several years, the Special Committee introduced resolutions delving into and condemning "military activities" in colonial territories as well as economic activities which were allegedly contrary to the best interests of the colonial peoples.[7]

Throughout all of this period in the Special Committee of Twenty-four, in the Trusteeship Council, and in both the General Assembly and the Security Council, the United States has tended to find itself in the middle on this issue of colonialism. In considering the issues in the United Nations, the United States has attempted to be a moderating factor, to discuss the issues logically and unemotionally, and, in general, to act in a responsible manner. This has, of course, resulted in dissatisfaction from both the colonialists and the anti-colonialists. The United States has advocated moderation, counselled measures which would lead to stability, and slow evolution toward independence through development of a sound economic, social, and political base. The Soviet Union has demanded instant emancipation, regardless of the situation. To the Soviets and the other anti-colonialists, the word "colonialism" is unequivocably bad, albeit imprecisely defined, and the word "self-determination" means one thing to one side and another to the other side.

In 1953 Assistant Secretary of State Henry A. Byroade endorsed "eventual self-determination for all peoples" and expressed his belief that "evolutionary development to this end should move forward with minimum delay." However, he pointed out, "premature independence can be dangerous, retrogressive and destructive."[8] In 1964 Ambassador Sidney R. Yates in his opening statement to the Special Committee in the United Nations said that U.S. foreign policy was dedicated toward helping to end colonialism by enabling dependent peoples to choose for themselves, freely and by democratic process, the type of government they wish.[9] This thinking was further confirmed by Vice President Humphrey in 1968 when he declared, "I wish to re-emphasize here and now my country's firm belief in the right of all men to live under governments of their own choosing."[10] He also noted that the United States has ". . . supported majority rule, human rights and self-determination throughout the world."[11]

The primary issue, then, is the definition of self-determination. As has been said, "The difficulties of self-determination become most serious when the doctrine is brought down from abstraction to working reality and when an effort is made . . . to translate it from ethical and political precepts to binding legal norms."[12]

In the United States's view, Puerto Rico and Guam have achieved self-determination. To the Soviet Union and the anti-colonialists, this is a sham, Rupert Emerson has stated that "The United Nations Charter speaks of the *principle* of self-determination: under what conditions can it be transformed into an operative *right?*"[13] He answers his own question by replying, "What emerges beyond dispute is that all peoples do *not* have the right of self-determination: they have never had it, and they never will have it. The changing content of natural law in the era of decolonization has brought no change in this basic proposition."[14]

As early as 1956 there had been considerable argument in the General Assembly between Administering Members and Non-Administering Members on the question of setting target dates for steps toward final achievement of full self-government. The United States finally arrived at a compromise and stated that it did not believe it would be useful to lay down long-range time limits but that the setting of intermediate target dates for political, social, and educational advancement could give a sense of purpose and direction to the peoples. The United States thus distinguished between intermediate and final goals for attainment of full self-government or independence.[15]

It is interesting to follow the change in philosophy on the part of both the United States and the Micronesians from the time of the Colonialism Declaration in 1960 to the present. In 1961 a request by the people of Saipan either to join with Guam or to become a separate U.S. territory was much discussed in the Trusteeship Council. The Trusteeship Council did not approve of either suggestion, because it felt the Territory should develop as a whole. The Department of the Interior also disapproved, because the Marianas had the highest standards and the best economy; if they separated themselves, the rest of the Territory would never be able to make a go of it.[16] No doubt, a strong feeling existed in the council in opposition to allowing the Territory to go to the United States piecemeal. The Council also noted that this unofficial plebescite did not fully reflect the basic objectives of Article 76 of the Charter. ("The basic objectives of the trusteeship system . . . shall be: . . . to promote the political, economic, social, and educational advancement of the inhabitants of the trust territories, and their progressive development towards self-government or independence. . . .")

The basic policy of the United States as Administering Authority of the Trust Territory was clearly established in 1962 by the Department of State, when it stated: "The policy . . . is to foster and encourage political advancement toward a goal of democratic self-government or independence. . . ." It placed the additional caveat that political development should be an evolutionary process.[17]

A year later, the U.S. Representative on the Trusteeship Council laid out the fundamental goals in the Trust Territory in these terms:

1. To raise the general level of health and education.
2. To build a productive economy enabling the people to achieve self-sufficiency and well-being.
3. To foster a sense of political unity and responsibility to enable the people to make an informed decision about their future.[18]

It might be noted that "independence" was not specifically mentioned. However, at the same time, the Department of the Interior was more specific, informing the Committee that "one of the duties imposed by the trusteeship agreement is to promote the progressive development toward self-government or independence. . . . Ultimately the peoples of the trust territory will choose their own destiny."[19]

The Visiting Mission of the Trusteeship Council in 1964 concluded that no fully matured opinions on the future of the Territory had yet emerged among the people of Micronesia. However, in spite of this conclusion, the Chairman of the Mission noted that "The Territory is reaching the point of political breakthrough; and this makes it possible to face up to the question of self-determination of Micronesia as a real rather than a hypothetical issue." The Visiting Mission further declared that the range of options for the future must start with independence and cover all other possibilities and urged the United States to plan a rapid advance of the Territory in all aspects of its political life. This recommendation was countered by the native representative to the Trusteeship Council, Mr. Remengesaus, who stated his misgivings over the stress on speed toward political growth irrespective of other factors. He concluded by arguing: "While speed of action may seem to some to be the important phase of political development at the present time, most of us feel that the present design of political growth through an evolutionary process, as expressed by the people themselves, is the most significant aspect."[20]

During this same 1964 session, the U.S. Representative to the Committee of Twenty-four recalled his earlier position that one of the most important questions was the "largely unexplored constitutional area which lies between sovereign independence and colonial dependency, namely, the small territories which are remnants of the colonial period." He further pointed out that the achievement of classical independence might not be practicable in a number of cases for non-self-governing territories.[21] And in the Council, Ambassador Yates stated "The people of Micronesia shall have the opportunity to exercise a free, informed, and meaningful choice concerning the type of government they wish for themselves and the nature of their future political associations."[22]

For the next few years, the representatives from the Congress of Micronesia to the Trusteeship Council expressed marked reluctance to rapid development toward political self-sufficiency. One such statement was: "Given several alternatives, the people invariably insisted that they wished to remain under the present system until they were ready. . . . The Micronesians are cautious and are reluctant to gamble for the price of uncertainty. When we are ready . . . we will ask for it."[23] Later, another native stated that the people of Micronesia did not want to exercise their right of self-determination until they had acquired first-hand knowledge of the possible alternatives available to them. Surprisingly, the Trusteeship Council warned that it would be premature to make any definite recommendations regarding the Territory's future status, since the precise timing of self-determination would depend largely upon the peoples' wishes expressed through the Congress of Micronesia.[24] This mild wording is in direct contrast to the harsher views of the Committee of Twenty-four, which felt that progress was not being made rapidly enough toward satisfying the requirements of the Colonialism Declaration.

The apparent watershed in the political status of the Trust Territory of the Pacific came in 1967 when President Johnson sent a message to Congress proposing the establishment of a status commission to recommend the best means of allowing the people of Micronesia to decide the future of the Territory. The Presidential proposal called for a plebescite to be held not later than 30 June 1972.[25] Shortly after this dramatic announcement the tenor of public pronouncements from Micronesian officials began to diverge from the party line which they and the U.S. officials had previously jointly issued concerning the status of American administration. The Micronesian Representative to the Trusteeship Council ominously proclaimed that there should be a reevaluation of the statement which had been made in 1967 that Micronesians were "not ready to exercise the rights of self-determination." With Nauru having achieved independence, he said, there was a need to reexamine the rate of progress toward self-determination; and consideration of independence had gained a new urgency.[26]

It is, perhaps, significant that this sudden reversal of attitude came about after the Micronesian Representative to the Trusteeship Council had become an elective office rather than an appointee by the U.S. authorities.

With the creation of the Status Commission, the propaganda barrage from the Communist bloc increased, and discussion of the subject in Congressional committees and elsewhere came under critical scrutiny. The Soviet Representative quoted Senator Mike Mansfield as saying that although the Pacific Islands were a Trust Territory, it was now unilaterally under the control of the United States.[27] The Iraqui Representative noted that the U.S. Secretary of the Interior had envisaged a "lasting political partnership" between the Territory and the United States. "Such an attitude," the Iraqi said, "was contrary to the right of self-determination." The Polish Representative added that the military presence of the United States in the Territory determined the future of the Territory to a certain degree, since there was little likelihood that the population could exercise complete liberty in its right to self-determination. Any solution other than association with the United States would be contrary to the openly declared military interests of the United States in the region.

The U.S. Representative's weak answer to the Soviet charge was that the Secretary's mention of a "lasting political partnership" with the United States only echoed the preliminary report of the Micronesian Future Political Status Commission. The Status Commission, selected by the popularly elected Congress of Micronesia, had stated in its report that the Micronesians chose an associated status because they recognized the historically unique partnership between Micronesia and the United States. They sought, he said, not an end but a redefinition, renewal, and improvement of the partnership.[28]

In mid-1969 Secretary of the Interior Hickel toured Micronesia, hoping to work out the outline of a new governmental plan for the Trust Territory with the Micronesian leaders prior to a plebescite. He stated at that time that the Nixon Administration would not offer a choice of whether the territory wanted independence or a stronger self-government, but rather, whether the Micronesians favored a new government.[29] This trip by the Secretary was marked by a number of governmental promises for the future of the Micronesians, for instance, more self-government, the upgrading of local participation in administration, and the payment of equal wages to Micronesians and Americans who do the same work. He said that the Administration would strive to make the economy more viable by expediting the development of roads, electric power, and other projects to improve the economic base. Further, legislation would be introduced in Congress in Washington to allow duty-free imports of Micronesian products.[30] All were measures which the Trusteeship Council and the Committee of Twenty-four had been asking for for years. Although President Johnson's legislative proposal to the U.S. Congress for a plebescite in 1972 was not passed that year and has not been enacted in succeeding years, that date of 1972 has stuck in the minds of the Micronesians, even though a plebescite seems to recede farther and farther into the future.

Mr. Hickel's statements must have fallen on receptive ears, or else the Micronesians simply rose to the occasion with pleasant speeches, for the answers to the Secretary's pledges were what the Americans wanted to hear. Senator Lazarus Salii, Chairman of the Status Commission, said that although "public opinion has been so opposed to the American Administration of the Trust Territory that the United States cannot take the Micronesians for granted, against a background of long colonial rule . . . most islanders strongly favor a permanent connection with the United States." Mr. Salii suggested that an early plebescite could endorse the union with the United States in principle, after which the details of the association could be worked out at a more leisurely pace, taking "perhaps five to eight years. There is a feeling of urgency that some decision must be made," he declared. "The uncertainty as to where we shall be in the future is becoming bothersome to more and more people every day."[31]

"Self-government is a perfectly possible proposition," said Neiman Craley, Assistant High Commissioner for Public Affairs, speaking in Saipan, "A Micronesian government need not necessarily come up to our standards evolved in 200 years to be effective."[32]

While friendly speeches were being exchanged in the islands, members of the Micronesian Congress were sounding a different warning in the United Nations. "The winds of change are beginning to blow, albeit still at zephyr strength," remarked Chutomu Nimwes. "Micronesia cannot begin to talk about developing its economic potentials," he declared, "until there are good roads between farms and market centers; until there is sufficient electricity to provide power to run machinery; until better water systems are installed to insure against seasonal water shortages; until better sewage systems have been provided to insure better sanitary conditions."[33]

The report of the Status Commission evidently envisages an eventual merger with Guam. In order to reach that condition it may be necessary to pass through a temporary condition of autonomy with a "free association" with the United States, since "it is unlikely that the United Nations would permit a direct and outright affiliation" of the two territories. The report noted that "many residents of all districts have come to look upon Guam as a source of education, transportation, employment and medical aid. Guam's degree of economic development as well as its very size and location render it difficult to ignore—particularly difficult for those who contemplate the political future of Micronesia."[34]

The advantages of a merger of the Trust Territory with Guam are not so clearly seen by the Guamanians. Politicians on Guam and Saipan put a plan for the merger of the Northern Marianas Islands with Guam to an unofficial vote in November 1969. The vote was merely a test of opinion and was not binding, but the Guamanians rejected the proposed affiliation by 3,720 to 2,688 in a light turnout. The adverse vote was ascribed partly to local resentment of the role in World War II of the Northern Marianas. Then they were ruled by Japan and residents of the islands were used by the Japanese for interpreters when they occupied Guam.[35]

The voters in the Marianas, on the other hand, voted in favor of the merger plan. The second most popular choice of the voters was to become part of a self-governing state of Micronesia in a "free association" with the United States. Only a few supported a proposal that the sixteen small islands of the group become an "unincorporated territory" of the United States, like Guam; and fewer still chose the alternative of belonging to an independent Micronesia.[36]

The Commission documented the preliminary announcement of its Chairman in July 1969 when it presented its final report to the Congress of Micronesia. In recommending that Micronesia should seek self-government in free association with the United States, it had patterned that concept on the definition outlined in Resolution 1541 (XV) of the General Assembly of the United Nations. The only alternative given to free association was complete independence. The Congress of Micronesia then approved the report of the Commission and appointed a new group—the Political Status Delegation—to examine further the problems of free association and independence.

At the invitation of Secretary of the Interior Walter J. Hickel, the Delegation proceeded to Washington to discuss the Trust Territory's political future, armed with an eleven-point list of critical issues. The U.S. representatives with whom the Micronesian delegation met generally agreed with Micronesia's basic position, but there were significant differences that could not be resolved immediately. At subsequent meetings, held in 1970, there were proposals and counter-proposals by both sides aimed at defining precisely future U.S.-Micronesian relationships. The specific relationship singled out for discussion was that of Commonwealth status, in free association with the United States. At the end of these discussions, despite recognized advantages to Commonwealth status, the Micronesian delegation nevertheless declared that ". . . the legal rights we consider essential to the effective protection of a Micronesian identity cannot be bartered for financial and economic advantages." The Commonwealth was rejected.

The alternative to free association advocated by the Micronesian Delegation was independence. After discussing the basic "rights" of the Micronesians to independence, the Delegation delved more explicitly into what this would mean to the islanders. The advantages would be primarily moral righteousness in deciding their own future. The disadvantages were viewed realistically as substantial, arising not from political considerations but from economic. To maintain even the present standard of living, Micronesia would need considerable assistance. It was recognized that an independent Micronesia might have difficulty in obtaining the initial financing necessary to develop a self-sufficient economy. And it was further recognized that the United States might be less likely to be responsive to requests for aid to an independent Micronesia then it might to a Commonwealth partner. As a final show of bravado, the Delegation pointed out that Micronesia might even declare independence unilaterally and outright.

The response of the United States representatives was disappointing to the Micronesians. Basically, the answer was that the United States did not consider independence to be a realistically appropriate status for Micronesia. The specific date for self-determination would "depend on the wishes of the Micronesian people and the ability of the United States, in good conscience and in accordance with its obligations under the Trusteeship Agreement, to agree that Micronesia is prepared for the choice in question." Thus was rung down the curtain on this attempt at settlement of the future political status of Micronesia.

Now, in 1972 the U.S. Government has come full circle in thinking about the future of Micronesia. The State Department and the Interior Department are both determined that the Trust Territories shall have a measure of self-government, preferably independence. The military services, just as in 1945, are still firmly convinced that the islands are vital to the future security of the United States. But now the situation is even more serious, in a military sense. Now, the United States faces a nuclear-armed China. Then, the enemy had just been defeated. Now, the U.S. position is facing a rollback from a forward stance. Then, the military bases in Japan, Okinawa, Korea, and the Philippines were firmly under U.S. control, to say nothing of the British and French positions in the Far East. For some time there has been a general feeling that the primary interest of the United States in Micronesia stems from military considerations—both a desire for bases and a need to deny the area to a potential enemy.

One school of thought proposes that the United States needs a whole complex of bases in the Pacific for the deployment of troops and logistic services to be used for conventional wars in Asia, for stockpiling nuclear weapons and missiles, and for the support and supply services to bombers and aircraft carriers.[37] Recently, the residents of the Palau Islands became concerned about military plans for their area and forwarded a resolution to the Trusteeship Council and the Security Council asking that the U.S. Marine Corps not establish the proposed training base in Palau. Lieutenant General Lewis Walt is reported to have promised that such a base would not be set up against the wishes of the islanders.[38]

More authoritative evidence of the views of the military concerning the value of the Trust Territory was given by Rear Admiral Lemos before a Senate sub-committee. According to his testimony, there are essentially three reasons why the Department of Defense considers the Territory important to the national security of the United States:

> The islands are strategically located, they could provide useful bases in support of military operations, and they provide valuable facilities for weapons' testing. Our continuing strategic requirements in the Pacific and our need to further develop United States missile capabilities will make the Trust Territory of the Pacific Islands increasingly valuable to the United States security interests in the area. . . . The islands are a natural backup to our forward bases in East Asia. Our major commitments in Asia and our deployments in the Western Pacific make it important that these islands be denied to potential enemies.

Thus, he said it was "in the vital interests of the United States" to continue political, economic, and social programs in the islands to provide an incentive to the islanders to "identify their desires and aspirations with ours." Through such a program, the Micronesians and the United States could work together toward mutually acceptable goals.[39]

Although there are still no military bases, as such, in the Trust Territory, the Micronesians are convinced that the United States is preparing to seize more land for military installations. Lending substance to these feelings is the pronouncement of Professor J. W. Davidson that "The genuine goodwill of United States officials towards Micronesia need not be questioned; but the fact that their government's primary interest in the islands has remained strategic seems to be established with singular clarity." His comments are particularly interesting when considering the state of mind of the Micronesian independence movement, because Professor Davidson is currently the constitutional adviser to the Congress of Micronesia. Formerly the constitutional adviser to the Government of Western Samoa (1959–61), to the Cook Islands Legislative Assembly (1963) and the Nauru Local Government Council (1967–68), he is more likely to advise the Micronesians toward independence than toward the Commonwealth status which the United States Government has proposed.

The dilemma for the United States is that the Government would most certainly like to be able to live up to its commitment to the United Nations and its long-announced adherence to the principle of self-determination. On the other hand, the physical security of the nation must remain the foremost consideration. The final outcome cannot be forecast with accuracy. A plan which might have been possible in the 1960s is no longer acceptable to both sides in the 1970s. The relations between nations is shifting. The political concepts of peoples, nations, and leaders are changing. But until the Micronesians feel that their economic and social future is guaranteed, and until the United States is assured that national security will not be jeopardized, there can be no final solution. One fact becomes apparent: the Micronesians expect continued financial support from the United States, no matter what the ultimate political settlement. In fact, the widespread call for immediate independence in recent years may in part have been an attempt to shock the American authorities into providing increased monetary resources to the Territory. On this side of the Pacific, however, it may be difficult to convince Congress to maintain even the present inadequate funding, for the Micronesians have no influential votes.

It is now beginning to look as if the Micronesians are indeed serious about calling for complete independence, even though they are fully aware that they do not have the necessary economic base for an independent and viable society without vast support from outside. In selecting this course, they would not be completely unique; for other small emerging nations in recent years have opted for complete political independence without any hope of becoming economically independent.

6 / American Involvement in Perspective

Lawrence E. Adams,

Colonel, United States Army

By the end of World War II there was overwhelming American consensus that Japan's former island mandates should remain under control of the United States because of their obvious strategic value. There were, however, major differences of opinion about how United States control should be exercised. While military leaders opted for annexation, the State Department argued for trusteeship under the United Nations. The compromise between these points of view produced the first and only United Nations strategic trusteeship, and the United States has administered this trust since 1947.

Today the future of the trusteeship is in doubt, and Micronesia is at a crossroads as the United Nations presses for the end of the trusteeship system and for self-government or independence in all trust and non-self-governing territories. The United States is understandably sensitive to criticism in its administration in Micronesia. During his term in office President Johnson proposed that the principle of self-determination be applied by means of a plebiscite to be held in Micronesia before 30 June 1972 and, ironically, the strategic value of Micronesia is likely to reach a new high about the same time. The American Congress and the Congress of Micronesia are currently studying the problem of Micronesia's political future and their forthcoming decisions will have an unquestionable impact upon American strategy in the troubled Pacific area.

The question "What is Micronesia?" was asked by *The New York Times* in a test of their readers' knowledge of current affairs in 1951. Although naval officers may have regretted the blank expression such a question drew from many Americans, Micronesia has since proved its international significance.

Today Micronesia is commonly used as a term synonymous with the Trust Territory of the Pacific Islands. There are certain differences between the two, the most notable being that the Micronesian island of Guam is a territorial possession of the United States and not a part of the trust territory. But for our purposes, use of the term *Micronesia* will refer only to the Trust Territory except when Guam is specifically included.

Micronesia is composed of more than 2,000 small islands divided into three major archipelagoes—the Marshalls, the Carolines, and the Marianas. These islands stretch above the equator from 1° to 20° north and from longitude 130° to 172° east. The Philippine Islands lie 500 miles to the west, Hawaii is approximately 1,800 miles to the east, and to the south are New Guinea and Australia. The encompassing ocean area of Micronesia is some 1,500 miles in width and 2,700 miles in length, or approximately the size of the continental United States. However, the total land area is less than 700 square miles which is considerably less than the state of Rhode Island. Literally, the term Micronesia aptly means "tiny islands." Almost everything about Micronesia is small except its value to American security and the distances between its islands, both of which are very great. The largest island in the trust territory is Babelthuap or Palau, located in the Carolines, with an area of 153 square miles. Most of the islands are small coral atolls. The people are scattered in several hundred villages on about 50 island clusters. Total population of the trust territory was 92,373 in 1966.

Micronesia first came to the attention of the western world in the 16th century. The Portuguese navigator Ferdinand Magellan discovered Guam in 1520 and although his voyage took him close to numerous other Micronesian islands he did not find them. Other Portuguese and Spanish explorers quickly followed in search of spices and gold. While Spain laid claim to these groups by right of discovery, she neglected them for over 300 years. Finally, in the late 19th century, Spain attempted to expand its administration. By this time explorers and traders of many nations had sailed the island waters and the Germans had developed a commercial interest in them. They had built up an active copra trade in the Marshalls and established a protectorate there in 1885. At first Spain questioned the German action, but the following year she recognized Germany's claim. The Carolines were also a matter of contention and there the Germans, using "gunboat diplomacy," claimed formal possession and the Spanish challenged it. War between these countries was avoided by submitting the dispute to Pope Leo XIII for adjudication. Spanish sovereignty was upheld with the condition that Spain establish an orderly government there.

The United States established its first claim in Micronesia in 1898. It acquired Guam along with the Philippines in the Spanish-American War after much debate and vacillation in Washington. President McKinley had considerable misgivings about the United States becoming a property owner in the western Pacific. However, a small but powerful group led by Theodore Roosevelt and Henry Cabot Lodge pressed hard for the so-called "large policy" to push America's destiny across the Pacific.

Admiral Dewey's famous naval victory in Manila Bay brought about a ground swell of public opinion in support of Pacific expansion. These factors, plus British encouragement, distrust of Germany, and the popular doctrines of Mahan, thrust the United States into the unfamiliar realm of Pacific politics and from that time forward, she has thought of herself as a Pacific power.

The line of American communications now stretched across the central Pacific from California through Hawaii, Wake Island, Guam, and the Philippines to China. However there was over 2,000 miles of water dotted with many islands outside the control of the United States. This potential threat caused little concern, probably because the nearby Marianas and Carolines were still under weak Spanish control. Unfortunately, a few months after the war, Spain sold all these island possessions to Germany for $4.2 million. Some American naval officers expressed alarm that the American line of communications was thus outflanked by the German possessions, but Admiral Mahan "saw no sufficient reason for our opposition."

Faced with this situation, the U.S. had to decide whether to take all the Marianas and the Carolines from Spain or not to take any of them. Roosevelt decided to take only Guam and the Philippines—a decision he later regretted. Roosevelt came to regret the decision as early as 1907, when he viewed the Philippines as America's "Achilles Heel" and thought the islands made our relations with Japan dangerous.

In 1914, at the outbreak of World War I, Japanese warships took possession of the German holdings in the Marshalls, Carolines and the Marianas, much to the consternation of the United States. Japan announced this acquisition was only temporary, but by secret agreement gained British support to retain the islands after the war. At the Faris Peace Conference, President Wilson fought a losing battle to free the former German colonies from Japan. The islands passed under Japanese control as a League of Nations Mandate.

In the development of Japanese policy during the interwar years, Micronesia's strategic value played an important part. The island chain greatly enhanced Japan's power and eventually served as the first line of defense against American and British naval forces. During the interwar years Japan's concern for her security steadily increased until her defensive strategy became overshadowed by the offensive and her growing preoccupation with national security was reflected in her policies relating to the islands. The Japanese were convinced that they lived in a hostile world and that the United States was a serious threat to their economic development and national expansion. They inhibited her drive for a widened economic base and her search for both raw materials and foreign markets.

In the years immediately following World War I, Japan did not expect to profit from the commercial value of Micronesia. The land areas were small, the distances were great, port facilities were totally inadequate, and, although the land was fertile, farming was difficult because of the problems of clearing the jungle land. Despite this, the Japanese government chartered corporations to undertake specific commercial projects and by 1922 there were about 40 such companies at work in Micronesia.

Japan's economic achievements were remarkable—sugar, phosphate, copra, pearls, and fish were exported in quantity. These achievements were made possible by the importation of over 70,000 Oriental colonists and workers in the 1930s. When necessary to maintain or increase production, the Japanese imposed forced labor upon the natives in a form of penal servitude called *karbos*. Remuneration to the Micronesians consisted of three meals a day in addition to a small monetary payment.

To carry out their responsibility as a mandatory, the Japanese established a civilian administration at Koror in the western Carolines. District administrations were also established, but political affairs were directly controlled by the Japanese with negligible local participation in government. In the middle thirties a radical change took place in Japanese politics as the military assumed the dominant role. Japan withdrew from the League of Nations and later began fortification of her island possessions but, as is pointed out in the following chapter, the fortification was less than was commonly believed. These events, added to the already strained relations, placed Japan and the United States on a collision course.

The Japanese attack against Pearl Harbor on 7 December 1941 initiated a nightmarish war in the Pacific which was to prove the great strategic value of the Micronesian islands. It was from these mandated island bases that Japan supported her driving offensive against the outflanked and vulnerable American outposts in the Pacific. Guam fell on 10 December, Wake Island on 23 December and Bataan surrendered in April 1942. Japanese forces rapidly spread out seizing Hong Kong, Singapore, Java, Borneo, Sumatra, and gravely threatened Midway, Australia, and Hawaii. The American defensive struggle to survive was greatly enhanced by her naval victory at Midway in June 1942. This watershed victory blunted the grand strategy of the Japanese offensive. But, the American counteroffensive now faced the monumental task of dislodging the Japanese from their strong island defenses which lay astride the American avenue of advance to the Japanese mainland.

The story of the American island-hopping offensive is well known and need not be told here. Suffice it to say that the tremendous costs of these island battles had the inevitable result of hardening American military thinking. American military leadership was dogmatically determined not to forfeit the fruit of their hard-won island victories. It was, in their opinion, absolutely essential that the Pacific Islands remain, after the war, under the full control of the United States. As late as October 1946 the Chief of Naval Operations, Admiral Chester W. Nimitz, appealed for United States sovereignty in the ex-Japanese mandate and felt that the concept of trusteeship was inapplicable to those islands because, in his view, they were politically insignificant and did not offer any economic advantage to the country administering them.[1]

During the war years the Joint Chiefs were given the broadest authority in the conduct of the war. The American tradition of separating military and political affairs was encouraged by President Roosevelt's disdain for formal coordinating machinery. He preferred to make the major decisions personally on controversial policies. There was minimal consultation between the military leadership and the Secretary of State. As a result, the political impact of strategic decisions tended to be neglected by the military planners. Secretary of State, Cordell Hull seemed to accept the principle of politico-military separation and remarked on the eve of the war to the Secretaries of War and Navy: "I have washed my hands of it and it is now in the hands of the Army and the Navy."[2]

Thus, while the Pentagon and the White House directed the conduct of the war, the State Department devoted its primary efforts to planning for the postwar world. Here, too, the planning was done in relative isolation and the distance across the Potomac River has never been greater. The primary thrust of this planning envisioned organizing world security around an international association similar to, but more powerful than, the League of Nations. It was anticipated that demands for independence and self-government by colonial peoples would be a major factor in the postwar years. Formal recognition of this fact was made in paragraph three of the Atlantic Charter signed 11 August 1941. As the war years went on and the concept of the United Nations became fully developed, the principle of trusteeship became inextricably involved. This principle, as it affected the Pacific Islands, became a source of inter-departmental, as well as Allied, dispute and is worthy of examination.

In November of 1943 President Roosevelt met with Churchill and Chiang Kai-shek at Cairo to discuss the war against Japan. At this meeting it was formally decreed that the mandated islands (and other territories as well) would be taken from Japan. This decision was announced in the Cairo Declaration:

> The Three Great Allies are fighting this war to restrain and punish the aggression of Japan. They covet no gain for themselves and have no thoughts of territorial expansion. It is their purpose that Japan shall be stripped of all the islands of the Pacific which she seized or occupied since the beginning of the First World War in 1914. . . . Japan will also be expelled from all other territories which she has taken by violence and greed.[3]

Upon his return to Washington, President Roosevelt commented to the Pacific War Council that control of the Japanese mandates should be exercised by the United Nations, but that security measures in the western Pacific, including control of necessary air and naval bases, should be exercised by those powers capable of exercising effective military control. One can speculate that the President clearly had the United States in mind as the guardian of peace in Micronesia.

In the months following the Cairo Conference, the State Department prepared a draft proposal for establishing trusteeship machinery in the United Nations Charter. It was intended that these procedures would be introduced by the United States at the Dumbarton Oaks Conference in September 1944. The draft proposal was submitted to the Joint Chiefs of Staff in June for their concurrence. The unfavorable military reaction to the proposal came from Secretary of the Navy Forrestal as he asked Under Secretary of State Stettinius, "if this [trusteeship draft] was a serious document and if he understood that the President was committed to it." He added, it seemed to him "there should be no debate on who ran the mandated islands."⁴ Secretary of State Hull argued: "It was not hard to see that Russia would not oppose outright [U.S.] acquisition to those islands, but it was also not hard to see that Russia would thereupon use this acquisition as an example and precedent for similar acquisition by herself."⁵

The Joint Chiefs took a strong position that the whole trusteeship question should await a U.S. policy determination on the ultimate disposition of the Japanese islands. Faced with this opposition, the Department of State agreed to withhold discussion of trusteeship from the Dumbarton Oaks Conference.

During the few months following the Dumbarton Oaks Conference there were numerous efforts to resolve the difference between the state and the military departments. These efforts were unsuccessful, and in January 1945 Secretary of War Stimson requested President Roosevelt to refrain from trusteeship discussions at the forthcoming Yalta Conference. Stimson argued that, "the larger powers who have won the war for law and justice will be obliged to maintain the security of the world which they have saved, during the time necessary to establish a permanent organization." Stimson viewed the Japanese mandated islands as essential to the United States's security and thought no trusteeship system should be devised until "the necessity of their [mandated islands] acquisition by the United States is established and recognized." Further, that it was evident to him the islands did not belong in the same trusteeship category as say the various German colonies.

. . . Acquisition of them by the United States does not represent an attempt at colonization or exploitation. Instead, it is merely the acquisition by the United States of the necessary bases for the defense of the Pacific for the future world. To serve such a purpose they must belong to the United States with absolute power to rule and fortify them. . . .[6]

In addition, Stimson warned that raising territorial issues at Yalta would probably result in a clash with the Soviet Union, who might demand a special relationship with Germany in the interest of her self-defense. Any such discussion should be avoided until the "Russians have clearly committed themselves" to the war against Japan.

Roosevelt recognized the advisability of avoiding territorial controversy at Yalta, but thought the establishment of the trusteeship principle was important to the establishment of the United Nations as a means to resolve such controversies. The United States therefore submitted at Yalta its ideas on providing international machinery for trusteeship.

When Stettinius reported to the three great allied leaders the U.S. proposal for dealing with territorial trusteeship, Churchill took exception. The Prime Minister said he did not agree with one single word of this report on trusteeship and that the British Empire would never be "put into the docks and examined by everybody." Stettinius then explained that the reference did not pertain to the British Empire, but, in particular, to the dependent territories taken from the enemy, such as the Japanese mandated islands. This seemed to satisfy Churchill, but he added that it would be better to specify that it did not refer to the British Empire.[7]

The Yalta Conference produced agreement among the great world powers on the principle of the United Nations. It now remained the task of the San Francisco Conference to write the U.N. Charter. The question of trusteeship was to be an essential part of the effort. As a prelude to the conference, an Inter-departmental Committee on Dependent Areas was formed and met in February 1945. Representatives from the Departments of Navy, War, Interior and State comprised the committee and to them was submitted a State Department redraft on the trusteeship system. It was found unacceptable to the military representatives and they suggested several specific changes: first, that trust territories should be of two types—strategic and non-strategic; second, that the Security Council rather than the General Assembly should have cognizance over "strategic trusteeships"; and third, that the "states concerned" should have final authority concerning selection of the administering authority and the terms of the specific trusteeship.[8] The substance of these amendments was reluctantly agreed to after several weeks of debate and the committee submitted their drafts to the department secretaries and the Joint Chiefs. On 9 March Roosevelt alarmed the Secretaries of War and Navy when he told them he had proposed to Stalin and Churchill that the Pacific Ocean areas be placed under "multiple sovereignty but that we would be requested by them to exercise complete trusteeship for the purpose of world security." Stimson remarked that if this idea was adopted, "the basis of our exercise of powers under it" should be "very clearly stated so that there could be no misunderstandings in the future."[9] Undoubtedly influenced by this discussion with the President, the military secretaries did not approve the trusteeship draft which had been concurred in by their representatives. The secretaries wanted no trusteeship talk in San Francisco until the United States officially announced its intentions to exercise full control over the strategic Pacific area. At the same time, the Secretaries of State and Interior felt that United States security could be safeguarded within the framework of the inter-departmental draft and that an attempt to exclude the Pacific Islands from discussion would make the United States appear guilty of having territorial ambitions. To resolve these differences, a meeting with the President was requested by the secretaries. Roosevelt agreed and set the date of 19 April but he did not live to keep the meeting. Because of Roosevelt's death and the desire to avoid forcing a decision on Truman, the new President, it was mutually agreed that the trusteeship question would be submitted to the United States Delegation in San Francisco for resolution. After considerable discussion, the delegation concluded a draft which generally met both military and civilian requirements. The draft dealt only with principles and international machinery making "no assumptions about the inclusion of any specific territory." Therefore, a public declaration by the United States reserving special rights in the Pacific was avoided. Eventual control of the Pacific Islands was still an open question. However, United Nations machinery was established at San Francisco which could protect United States interests if and when the Pacific Islands were offered for trusteeship.[10]

In August 1945 fighting in the Pacific ceased. At this time, the Navy controlled most of the former mandated islands. The same month, President Truman designated the Secretary of the Navy as interim administrator of the islands. The Navy moved rapidly to bring previously bypassed areas under its control. In October the President appointed a high level committee consisting of the Secretaries of State, War, Navy, and Interior to study the problems of future administration of the islands and make appropriate recommendations to him. These postwar discussions reopened the old arguments for annexation versus trusteeship and introduced the new question of which U.S. department would exercise administrative control. At this point, the military departments themselves were in disagreement, and while they agreed on full United States control, they differed on who should exercise it.

In September 1945 it was mutually agreed between the military departments that their differences would be resolved before entering into discussions with the State Department. At this time, the Joint Staff felt that "the strategic responsibility for the area was an indivisible whole and that the bases should be part of an integrated system to facilitate the defense of the United States. Therefore, since its defense was a common mission of the Army and the Navy, the Joint Chiefs of Staff shall have the strategic responsibility. . . ."[11]

On 10 January 1946 the first session of the General Assembly of the United Nations met in London. On 15 January the new Secretary of State, James Byrnes, who was attending the conference, sent a cable to Washington requesting permission from the President to make a statement that the United States would be prepared to place the former mandated islands "either under ordinary trusteeship arrangements or as strategic areas." Acting Secretary of State Acheson obtained the President's approval but failed to coordinate with the military departments. On 21 January, upon learning of these messages, the Secretary of the Navy and the Under Secretary of War called upon the President. They informed him that they thought it was an unwise decision and requested the President to instruct Byrnes not to make the statement. The President reported that a message had been sent "requesting Byrnes not to commit this country to any definitive position." Forrestal remarked in his diary:

This incident is a reflection of the rapidly vanishing determination in America to see to it that we do not repeat the mistakes of 1918–19 when the formerly German-owned islands of the Pacific were turned over to Japan and Australia—those north of the equator to Japan, those south to Australia—under a secret agreement between England and Japan without American knowledge until it was a *fait accompli*. It is a case for the greatest concern to see this tendency developing so soon in the attitude of the State Department.[12]

In February 1946 it was publicly announced that Southern Sakhalin and the Kurile Islands would be awarded to Russia as a part of the Yalta agreements. This announcement created a new round of public and congressional clamor for United States annexation of the Pacific Islands. The debate continued on through the summer of 1946 with much heat and little light. The military continued to argue for complete annexation, the State Department for trusteeship and the Interior Department for administrative control whatever the islands' status.

Secretary of the Interior Ickes was dead set against naval administration of the Pacific Islands and was highly critical of past Navy performance in Guam and Samoa. He was joined in an anti-Navy campaign by Mr. John Collier, President of the Institute of Ethnic Affairs. On 29 May 1946 Secretary Ickes delivered a speech in Washington in which he alleged:

> The Navy is bent upon ruling these island people and it is determined that they shall not have those rights which the Charter of the United Nations guarantees; that they shall not have self-government or democracy or racial equality. . . . Naval absolutism sneers at every Constitutional guarantee. . . . The Navy is arbitrary, dictatorial and utterly disregardful of civilian rights. . . . Grotesque, inefficient, tyrannical not wantonly cruel, but faithless to pledges given—such has been naval rule over subject peoples.[13]

Mr. Collier also joined in the anti-Navy campaign, and *The New York Times* became the battleground for Collier's charges of Navy misrule and Secretary Forrestal's reply that the Navy's record "needs no defense" but that the democratic rights of the islands' inhabitants was the "exact objective of naval civil government and, for that matter, of military government as well."[14] Later, in 1946, Ickes resigned as Secretary of the Interior, but used his newspaper column to renew the feud between the Departments of the Navy and the Interior. Secretary Forrestal recorded his impression of Mr. Ickes' attack in a private memorandum which he quietly filed away:

> High in the moral stratosphere, Mr. Ickes, bathed in the serene light of his own self-approval, emanating the ectoplasm of conscious virtue, views the motive of most men as mean and vulgar, with, of course, one notable exception . . . for tolerance, understanding, wisdom and devotion to the cause of human freedom. I believe the Admirals, when called upon for their final accounting before their maker will not have to step aside, unless Harold Ickes does it by force.[15]

Despite the heated but rather isolated criticisms, the Navy Department continued to exercise military government in the mandated islands until 18 July 1947 and even then continued the civil administration until 29 June 1951.

In October 1946 President Truman called a meeting to discuss the future of the Pacific Islands. The State and War Department representatives had by this time agreed that because Japan had received the islands from the League of Nations under a mandate, the rights of the United States were not superior to those delegated by the League and, therefore, the United States should declare them a strategic area to be administered by them under a trusteeship agreement. According to Secretary Byrnes, "the Secretary of the Navy was very reasonable and did not want us to do anything that would show lack of confidence in the United Nations."[16] Thus, the President made his decision, and on 6 November 1946 announced: "The United States is preparing to place under trusteeship, with the United States as the administering authority, the Japanese mandated islands and any Japanese islands for which it assumes responsibility as a result of the Second World War. . . ." He went on to add that a draft of the strategic area trusteeship agreement was being sent to other members of the Security Council. On 26 February 1947 Ambassador Warren R. Austin submitted to the Security Council the United States draft agreement accompanied by a brilliant but lengthy article by article explanation of the American viewpoint. The American proposal did not meet any substantial opposition in the Security Council and although several amendments were offered, only three minor amendments and two changes were made. On 2 April 1947 the Security Council voted unanimously for approval and on 18 July the American Congress, by joint resolution, approved it.

Thus, the long debate over the fate of the Micronesian islands was resolved. The approved trusteeship agreement had met the primary causes of the American debate in the following manner. The military departments' primary concern for United States security was recognized by designating the trust territory as a strategic area (Article 1); the United States was designated as the sole administering authority (Article 2); with full powers of administration, legislation, and jurisdiction over the territory including application of U.S. laws as appropriate (Article 3); and the

United States was entitled to establish "naval, military and air bases" with the stationing and employment of armed forces in the territory (Article 5).

The political and humanitarian objectives were recognized in that the United States agreed to the development of local political institutions as a step toward self-government or independence; to promote the economic development, social advancement, health, education and fundamental rights and freedom of the population (Article 6); to grant freedom of speech, press, assembly, worship and migration (Article 7); and to take "necessary steps to provide the status of citizenship" for Micronesians (Article 11).

The Department of the Navy administered the trust territory until 1 July 1951 when the responsibility was transferred to the Secretary of the Interior. In 1952 and 1953 certain of the northern Marianas were returned to Navy control for reasons of security, but in May 1962 President Kennedy again placed them under the administration of the Secretary of the Interior.

Although American control of the trust territory is almost unrestricted under the sweeping terms of the trusteeship agreement, in recent years the United States has been under increasing pressure from the United Nations to expedite its responsibility to promote the "progressive development toward self-government or independence of the territory." Most of this pressure has been initiated by the Soviet Union. In December 1960 the General Assembly passed Resolution 1514 (XV), which had been proposed by Nikita Khrushchev. This resolution proclaimed "the necessity of bringing to a speedy and unconditional end colonialism in all its forms and manifestations."[17] The following month the United States announced its intention to abide by the essence of the resolution through progressive steps of political development in the Trust Territory of the Pacific.

The Trusteeship Council is also involved in questions concerning Micronesia. Article 83 of the United Nations Charter provides that strategic areas are under the cognizance of the Security Council. The same article provides that the Security Council shall, "without prejudice to security. considerations, avail itself of the assistance of the Trusteeship Council to perform those functions of the United Nations under the trusteeship system relating to political, economic, social and educational matters in the strategic areas." Despite Soviet pressure, the Trusteeship Council has generally maintained a reasonable position on the question of self-determination in Micronesia. While urging the United States to take all possible steps leading to self-determination, it has shown a general awareness that Micronesia is not yet ready or willing to make this far-reaching political decision. Undoubtedly, this attitude has been conditioned by the western membership on the Council as well as by committee visits to the islands. The Soviet Union attempted to force the issue in July 1966 by introducing a resolution to set a deadline date for Micronesian self-determination. This resolution was soundly defeated.[18]

In August 1967 President Johnson asked the American Congress to choose members to constitute a Presidential Commission to consider with him the future status of the trust territory and determine the desirability of calling a plebiscite before 30 June 1972. This proposal was received with mixed emotions in Micronesia. Although Micronesians are eager to learn what political options Washington might offer, many reportedly believe that 1972 is "too early" for a plebiscite. Some evidence indicates that most Micronesians would prefer some sort of union with the United States. However, some of the older elements of the society have fond memories of the former Japanese administration. The United States could hold a plebiscite in Micronesia at any time but it would be of limited value unless the people knew its purpose. Today they would probably vote for the *status quo*. An educational process to inform the native people is required before a meaningful plebiscite can be held. Micronesia's preparedness for self-determination is directly related to the progress of the United States in carrying out its obligations for the development of the territory. This leads us to an examination of the Trust Territory of the Pacific as it exists today.

Primary American base development in Micronesia has taken place in Guam, which is not a part of the trust territory. From this island both Strategic Air Command and naval aircraft are launched in support of the war in Vietnam. In addition, Guam's naval base provides logistic support to the Pacific Fleet. The numerous World War II airfields built throughout the islands have, for the most part, been reclaimed by nature. But Kwajalein in the Marshall Islands provides a major trans-Pacific airfield for both military and civilian air traffic and, in addition, provides test range facilities for ballistic missiles and space vehicles.

Previously, the islands of Bikini and Eniwetok both in the Marshall

Islands were used for American nuclear testing. This program drew sharp criticism from the Marshallese people and the United Nations. The Soviet Union and India, in particular, raised the nuclear issue each year in the Trusteeship Council, but the United States defended its testing on the grounds of military necessity. An unfortunate incident occurred during the 1954 tests when a hydrogen bomb yielded unexpected radioactive fallout which forced the evacuation of 236 islanders from Uterik and Rongelap atolls. Although a number of these people suffered physical injury, all have apparently recovered.

Probably the greatest advantage which the trust territory provides to American security is that of denial of the islands to an unfriendly power. United States control of these largely unfortified islands insures her free movement across the Pacific and provides a partial barrier along the U.S. sea line of communication. If United States forces are withdrawn from the Asian mainland, Micronesia would become vitally important as a strategic forward position. Such a position could support a variety of widely spread U.S. reaction forces, compounding the targeting problems of a potential enemy, as well as providing a major psychological deterrent to Chinese aggression in Asia. Aside from the quick reaction potential, the islands are strategically important as wartime logistic bases. The vast number of deep-water lagoons provides dispersed anchorage particularly useful in a nuclear environment. Submarine and anti-submarine warfare in the western Pacific could be effectively supported from any number of the islands. The trust islands remain a valuable, if undeveloped asset to the national security of the United States.

Under the provisions of Article 76 of the United Nations Charter, the United States has the responsibility to promote the "progressive development toward self-government or independence" of the territory. In fulfillment of this long-term objective, the United States has taken steps in the progressive political, economic, and social development of Micronesia.

Political development has been from the bottom up. First municipal governments were established, then district legislatures and finally in 1965 a territorial legislature—the Congress of Micronesia. The transition to democratic processes has been particularly difficult in those areas where hereditary leadership was traditional. In the beginning hereditary leaders were automatically elected to office, but today this practice is losing ground to political campaigning. Micronesian legislation remains subject to the approval of the United States High Commissioner. Nevertheless, this experience in democratic government appears to be a dramatic step toward eventual self-government.

Economic development has been slow and difficult. Subsistence farming and fishing remain the base of the economic structure. A money economy exists only in a few semi-urbanized areas. Copra, World War II scrap metal, fish and handicraft constitute the bulk of a limited foreign export. National income has risen from $5.5 million in 1962 to $10.7 million in 1966. The cost of trust territory operations in 1967 was met primarily through a $25 million appropriation from the United States Government. In recent years limited private investment capital has been introduced; for example several hotels and motels have been constructed in response to a growing tourist trade. In an effort to expedite economic growth, the United States has hired an economic consultant to study and report on all feasible means of resource development. The promotion of tourism seems a worthwhile objective. The United Nations Trusteeship Council has been critical of the rate of economic development and is "convinced that independence from external aid" can be achieved through development of island agriculture and industry.

Social advancement in the territory is difficult to measure in terms of the western world. An effort is being made to integrate new ideas into the Micronesian culture without destroying it. To promote general education, a free public school system has been established. In 1966 over 80% of the territory's children, aged 7 to 14 years, were attending schools and approximately 300 students were graduated from high school. Teaching is in English and primarily conducted by American teachers. A major goal is the training of Micronesian teachers and toward this end a teachers' education center has been established in Ponape. Higher education is centered primarily in Guam, and in 1966, 257 students from the territory were enrolled at the college level.

Medical service in Micronesia is a scarce commodity and modern medical facilities are limited to those provided by the government. District hospitals serve the semi-urban areas; however, the inhabitants of the outer islands receive infrequent medical care through field visits. There is a major shortage of medical personnel. As of June 1966 there were only five medical doctors, all non-indigenous, and thirty-two indigenous medical practitioners. The United Nations has been highly critical of the medical program and a recent investigation by the World Health Organization revealed numerous deficiencies. Despite the doctor shortage, public health measures have brought a rising birth rate and falling death rate, and the population has doubled in 20 years.

In our analysis of Micronesia, we come to the vital question: Has the strategic trusteeship adequately served American national security? The answer appears to be yes. Of course, these islands provide no defense to the United States against an attack by intercontinental ballistic missiles. They do, however, have a potential as widely dispersed missile sites, airfields, and naval bases. Today development of such sites is considered neither strategically necessary nor economically and politically feasible. It remains simply an option, but in a rapidly changing world such options are valuable insurance against the future.

7 / Japan and the Mandates

Paul B. Haigwood,

Colonel, United States Marine Corps

"The Army's Pearl Harbor Board linked the disaster of December 7, 1941, directly to our failure to have a showdown with Japan on her fortifications of the mandated islands."[1] This sentence from the biography of Charles Evans Hughes is typical of a number of American sources which directly or by implication accused Japan of violating her international treaties and fortifying the mandated islands during the 1920s and 1930s.

In examining the origins of the Pacific War, one of the more interesting aspects is whether or not Japan did fortify the Marianas, Marshalls, and Caroline Islands during this period or was fortification a myth brought about by speculative writings.

The purpose of this chapter is to examine the available sources and attempt to determine the truth concerning this era of history.

The Japanese mandated islands consist of 1400 islands and coral reefs known as the Marianas, the Carolines, and the Marshalls. If an imaginary rectangle were placed about them its dimensions would be 1200 miles from north to south and 2500 miles from east to west. The northern group, the Marianas, lie 1200 miles south of Yokohama, Japan; the Carolines are an insular belt just north of the equator; and the Marshalls lie about midway between the Hawaiian Islands and the Philippines. Despite these impressive figures, the actual land area is only 836 square miles, one-seventh the size of the Hawaiian Islands. Although the islands are small and widely scattered, of limited economic value, and far from the conventional avenues of the world's maritime commerce, their strategic location is extremely important to the balance of naval power in the Pacific.

These islands, which belonged to Germany prior to World War I, were mandated to Japan as a part of the Versailles Peace Treaty. Article 4 of this mandate directed:

> The military training of the natives, otherwise than for purposes of internal police and the local defense of the territory, shall be prohibited. Furthermore, no military or naval bases shall be established, or fortifications erected in the territory.[2]

The system of which this mandate was a part was a compromise between annexation and internationalization. Thus, Japan received not the territorial right to the former German islands, but rather an international trust subject to supervision by the League of Nations.[3]

In addition to the terms of the mandate, which denied Japan the right to fortify the islands or build bases there, three arrangements affecting the mandate islands were made at the Washington Disarmament Conference. These were:

> 1. A ten-year non-aggression treaty in regard to the islands in the Pacific, by which in reality a four-power agreement (United States, Japan, British Empire, and France) was substituted for the Anglo-Japanese Alliance.
>
> 2. A five-power (United States, Japan, British Empire, France, and Italy) agreement to maintain the status quo with regard to fortification and naval bases until 31 December 1936.
>
> 3. A Japanese-American treaty by which the United States agreed to the mandate, obtained for itself the same rights as a member of the League, and full privileges in regard to the use of Yap for cable and radio installations. Japan also assured the "usual comity" to American nationals and vessels visiting the islands.[4]

Thus, the Japanese were prohibited from fortifying the mandated islands by both the League of Nations and the Washington Naval Conference treaties. Furthermore, in order to have some means of checking by first hand observation whether or not the Japanese were living up to their promises, the United States had negotiated a separate treaty with Japan on 11 February 1922 which committed the Japanese to permit American vessels and American nationals to visit the islands.[5]

From the beginning of Japanese occupation of the islands in 1914, there was considerable suspicion in naval circles that the islands were being prepared for naval use. During World War I the Japanese even excluded ships of their British ally, and after the war, despite agreement with the Allies and the United States in Washington, they excluded foreign ships.[6] As the Admiral of the United States Asiatic Fleet pointed out in 1915, the Japanese had been very clever in the way they excluded ships. The rule was merely that no ship could visit the islands without permission, but all steamers bound for the islands had to clear from Yokosuka, a port which was barred to foreigners.[7]

During this period of time (between the end of World War I and the beginning of the Washintgon Naval Conference), the Director of United States Naval Intelligence, Rear Admiral Roger Welles, fearing activities dangerous to the United States, suggested that an officer from Guam go for a "health trip" through the neighboring islands.[8] Admiral Welles's suggestion opened the door for the now-famous escapades of Lieutenant Colonel Peter Ellis to take place. Known in Marine Corps circles as the master strategist and spy, Ellis is said to have waged a single-handed war against the Japanese Empire.

Lieutenant Colonel Ellis was ordered to report to Headquarters Marine Corps in July 1920 and was assigned a special classified project by the Commandant, General Lejeune. The project had been closeted for almost a year when Ellis produced a 30,000 word document entitled "Advanced Base Operations in Micronesia." This document, which was classified "Top Secret" and approved as "Operation Plan 712-H" by Commandant Lejeune, predicted war between the United States and Japan. Major points of his predictions were:

> Japan would initiate a war against the United States. Japan's objectives in launching an attack would be Hawaii, Wake, Midway, Guam, and the Philippines. It was dangerous to give Japan control over the mandate islands. The United States counter-attack plan, after the Japanese initial strike, called for seizure of key islands in the Marshall and Caroline Islands. These objectives would be necessary to provide the fleet with bases from which to launch a counter-attack against the Philippines. The eventual advance on the Japanese homeland would have to be made via the Marianas and Bonin Islands.[9]

The writing of Operation Plan 712-H and its accurate predictions concerning the beginning of World War II in the Pacific and United States strategy against Japan were not the end of the Ellis story. Although the information is sketchy and partially unconfirmed, Ellis is thought to have spent more than two years in the Carolines, in the guise of a drunken trader, who was in the service of United States Naval Intelligence. His exact mission is unknown, but evidence indicates he was attempting to confirm his suspicions regarding fortification. The Japanese reported his death in the Carolines on 12 May 1923.[10] Captain Ellis M. Zacharias, United States Navy, head of the office of Naval Intelligence in Tokyo during the 1920's, confirms a portion of the Ellis story and tells an even more bizarre story of the Navy enlisted man who was sent to pick up the body of Lieutenant Colonel Ellis.[11]

In 1921 and 1922, both before and after the Washington Naval Conference, the Japanese protested vigorously against the appearance of American planes in the vicinity of Rota near Guam. In responding to the Japanese protest, Admiral Robert Edward Coontz, Chief of Naval Operations, showed that he had not lost his sense of humor when he wired the Governor of Guam ". . . every care should be exercised in the selection of carrier pigeons so that . . . they will return to Guam instead of landing on Rota."[12]

Public opinion was so optimistic about the outcome of the Washington Naval Conference that people tended to believe that the Japanese were acting in good faith in all matters. In view of this situation, the Navy's suspicions that a problem existed in the mandated islands received no known official support outside military circles. In fact, accounts of far eastern matters available to the public, both official and unofficial, tended to affirm Japanese good faith. In 1923 former Assistant Secretary of the Navy Franklin D. Roosevelt declared, in answer to his own question, "Shall we trust Japan?", that Japan was not only living up to the letter, but to the spirit, of the (Five Power) treaty. If, instead of looking for causes of offense, we in all good faith confidently expect from Japan cooperation in world affairs, we shall go forward insuring peace.[13]

The concensus of Americans, up to the time of the Manchurian crisis, was that the Japanese were our friends and were committed to peace.[14]

With this public and official attitude, it was very difficult for the Navy to elicit enthusiasm from the State Department when they requested that permission be obtained for naval vessels to visit the mandated islands. Dorothy Borg, an authority on American policy in the Pacific in the interwar years, reports in her writings that throughout the 1920s the State Department made no more than "half-hearted" efforts to get permission for the United States Navy to send ships into the islands for visits. The

Japanese paid little attention and took no action to these requests.[15] At each attempt by the State Department to gain permission for U.S. vessels to call at ports in the mandated islands, the Japanese indicated their opposition and the State Department dropped the issue without protest. The American Government, Miss Borg concludes, "abided by the wishes of the Japanese throughout the next years."[16]

The chronology of developments concerning the mandate next took the form of charges in the press that the Japanese were fortifying the islands and preparing them for war.[17] As a result of these charges, the Mandates Commission of the League of Nations carefully questioned the Japanese Representative, Mr. Ito, in both 1932 and 1934 concerning their annual reports.

Though the Mandates Commission had strong suspicions that Japan was violating the terms of the mandate, the evidence was largely circumstantial; and since officials of the League of Nations lacked authority to visit territories under mandate, corroborating evidence could not be obtained.[18] The United States was handicapped by not belonging to the League of Nations and by the absence of an American on the Mandates Commission. However, the United States did make informal contacts with the Commission via the American Embassy in Rome and the Italian Chairman of the Mandates Commission.[19]

In questioning the Japanese representative, the Commission indicated that they were concerned that Japan was spending over three times more on "harbor improvements" than earlier. The chairman of the Commission was quoted as saying that "a naval base was not self-evident and could be disguised as harbor works."[20] Mr. Ito, the Japanese representative, stated that the rumors were unfounded, but the Commission was not satisfied. They invited Japan to show conclusively that the projects she was undertaking were simply for commercial use and generally to refute the charges made against her. The Japanese government backed up Mr. Ito with a letter, but the Commission was not convinced. However, there were no threats against Japan. The Commission could not send observers and Japan knew this. Sharpness of questions and requests that Japan include more information in next year's report was as far as the Commission was willing and able to go. The exchange between Mr. William Rappard and Mr. Ito is fairly typical of the questions and the fencing that occurred.

Although the Japanese did not fair too well with the Mandates Commission, nothing was done. The more consuming question was Manchuria and what Japan was going to do on the mainland of China. On 27 March

1933 Japan gave notice of her withdrawal from the League of Nations which became effective two years later. Huntington Gilchrist, writing in *Foreign Affairs*, summed up world opinion concerning Japan and her mandate of the Pacific Islands after her notice to withdraw from the League of Nations.

> There was much unofficial discussion of Japan's right to continue as a Mandatory Power, but no member of the League raised the question officially. Japan's annual reports continued to arrive in Geneva for a few years more, but in 1938 she ceased to collaborate with the League. Significantly, the final report submitted (late in 1939) failed to contain the usual paragraph to the effect that Japan had not constructed fortifications or bases in the islands.[21]

In addition to the publications and press coverage of the Mandates Commission suspicions, the United States Government was itself receiving information through its representative in Japan that the Japanese might be fortifying Yap, Saipan, and Palau. In March 1933 Ambassador Joseph Grew wrote:

> There was abundant first hand evidence that Japan was engaging in military preparations on the mandated islands and that the whole problem of fortifications on the islands was full of potential dynamite and might yet cause as much trouble as Manchuria.[22]

In spite of these storm signals, the Roosevelt administration approached the subject of refusal of access to the mandated islands very cautiously. The first time the issue was raised with Ambassador Saito was in June 1934 when the Ambassador was about to depart on a brief visit home. Miss Borg reports the following events: a conversation between the representative of the State Department and the ambassador in which the latter was requested to explore the possibility of greater American access to the mandated islands in order to remove suspicions of Japanese fortification. After consultation with naval authorities in Japan, the ambassador stated that they "were prepared to grant any request for foreign naval vessels to cruise among the mandated islands freely and enter any port they wished."[23]

In spite of these assurances the United States did not submit any requests for naval vessels to visit the islands until two years later, in 1936. When requests for the USS *Alden* and the USS *Gold Star* to visit Saipan, Truk, and Palau on certain dates in 1936 were turned down, the United States submitted alternate dates which were also refused. During the same period, the British were denied permission for British naval vessels to visit the mandates on the grounds that it was "inconvenient for some time to come."[24] In addition to denial of the American and British requests, it is significant to note that after 1937 the Japanese did not allow any foreign ships to visit Micronesia.[25]

In summary, the Roosevelt administration's handling of the problem of the Pacific Islands played an important part in the formation of its Far Eastern policy. As far as the mandates were concerned, it is quite evident that the State Department deliberately abstained from probing into the question of fortifications because it wished to avoid a controversy with the Japanese. In dealing with United States-owned insular possessions in the Pacific, the Roosevelt administration decided to adhere to the status quo (non-fortification) of its own islands even after the Washington Naval Treaty lapsed in 1936. This decision ran counter to the wishes of both the Army and the Navy, but from all appearances President Roosevelt and Secretary Hull and his advisers were opposed to the construction of fortifications and bases in the West Pacific primarily for political reasons, foremost among which was the desire to avert trouble with Japan.[26]

Charles Evans Hughes's biographer was most critical of the way the Roosevelt administration handled the issue of the Japanese mandated islands. He wrote:

> In 1939 Secretary Hull admitted to the Senate Committee on Naval Affairs that the Japanese authorities had denied every request (four in number) that the department had made for the privilege of visiting harbors and waters of the mandated islands. At the same time he asked the committee to keep this information secret. Under hush-hush precautions, the State Department replied to another query . . . that the Government of the United States has at no time raised any question with the Japanese Government in regard to the obligations of Japan to the United States with respect to the Japanese mandated islands.[27]

Thus, it appears that the rights of visitation that former Secretary of State Hughes had so carefully safeguarded and negotiated during the Washington Naval Conference of 1922 was surrendered by subsequent administrations. The Army's Pearl Harbor Board complained about the apparently lax way in which the United States chose to wink at treaty violations. With the benefit of hindsight, American officials speculated that, had the United States insisted on the fulfillment of treaty stipulations, Japan's military build-up in the Pacific would have been made impossible. Instead, the Japanese were given a free hand to develop the islands and exclude everyone except nationals of Japan.

As a consequence of the foregoing, Japan gained enormous advantage of a string of naval and air and army bases across our lifeline to the Philippines and rendered futile and impotent any fortification of our own islands, such as Guam, Midway, Christmas, Palmyra, etc. It also placed the dagger's point at the heart of the Hawaiian Islands because such a base at Jaluit in the mandated islands was a thousand miles closer to Hawaii than to the homeland of Japan.[28]

While it appears to be true that the United States deliberately abstained from probing into the question of fortifications because it wished to avoid a controversy with the Japanese, there is no "hard" evidence that the islands were actually fortified prior to Japan's withdrawing from the League of Nations and the expiration of the Washington Naval Conference restrictions in 1936.

Professor Paul H. Clyde, an assistant professor of history at Ohio State University from 1925 through 1931, was allowed to visit a number of the mandated islands in 1933–1934. His findings indicate that there had been an improvement in a number of harbors (Saipan and Truk), construction of an airfield on Saipan, and erection of oil storage tanks at several locations; but he and his associates saw no evidence of military preparations or fortifications.[29] Willard Price's book, *Japan's Islands of Mystery*, confirms Professor Clyde's observations. He states:

Japan did not build great fortifications, not because the mandate forbade such installations, but because they were not needed. . . . In the sense of natural fortifications of reefs, cliffs, marshes, etc., the islands are heavily fortified. In addition, many of the islands are perfect bases for destroyers and submarines, and are naturally built aircraft carriers.[30]

Most of the construction projects observed by both Clyde and Price and discussed at the League of Nations could be attributed to the commercial growth in the islands. Huntington Gilchrist provided the following statistics regarding economic growth under the Japanese:

Trade was 20 times greater in 1936 than 1917. In 1936 it exceeded $22 million, or more than $200 per head of population. In 1914, the sugar cane industry did not exist; by 1936 its exported value was $6.5 million per year.[31]

The Japanese position regarding fortification of the Marianas, Marshalls, and Carolines basically was not known until after the end of World War II. Of course, their answers to the Mandates Commission of the

League of Nations received wide publicity during the 1930s, but there was no proof of the Japanese innocence. The tight security that had been in effect since 1914, coupled with the "foot dragging" on requests concerning visitation by naval vessels and correspondents, tended to make the world suspicious of the Japanese. After the wide press coverage of the Manchurian incident, most nations and the world public were prepared to believe the worst. The Japanese attempted to partially overcome this image by inviting Professor Clyde and a few other selected visitors to travel through the mandates during the 1930s, but this was not a full-scale effort. Therefore, the Japanese story was not known until after World War II when the eleven nation Allied Military Tribunal delved into the question of fortification.

Lieutenant General Masatake Okumiya (Ret.), wrote an article for the United States Naval Institute *Proceedings*, which outline an impressive answer to the question. Highlights of his research are discussed hereafter as a balance for the American position, or at least suspicion, that Japan violated treaties by fortifying her mandated islands before World War II.

First, Okumiya confirms in his writing that the Imperial Navy did occupy the islands from 1914 until 1921, but immediately after the Washington Naval Conference the Nanyo Kohatsu Agency, a private business corporation, with all stock shares in public hands, was established for the purpose of governing and developing the mandated islands. The Imperial Navy did retain the responsibility for security of the area, but this was carried out by one naval attache and a few assistants.[32]

The rumors that regular Japanese military units were stationed in the mandated islands during the 1920s and 1930s have been denied by Japanese sources. Imperial Army Colonel Susumu Nishiura states the following regarding army forces:

> The first regular Japanese military outfit to enter the zone was the XXXI Army Corps, whose five divisions of troops spread over Guam, Saipan, Tinian, Truk, and a few other islands in 1944. Not a single Kempeitai and not a single Army soldier was assigned to Saipan until 1943. A token Kempeitai unit (military police) for the mandated area was activated in 1943.[33]

Although these comments were intended to counter the claim that military police units operated in Saipan in 1937, it indicates that the Japanese Army neither fortified nor conducted maneuvers in the mandated islands during the 1920s and 1930s.

With regard to the stationing of regular naval units, Vice Admiral Suguru Suzuki, former commander-in-chief of the Maritime Self-Defense Force's Defense Fleet, stated:

> As an Imperial Navy lieutenant commander serving at the Information Section of the wartime Naval Chief of Staff, I testified at the 11-nation Allied Military Tribunal at Tokyo in 1947, denying the allegation that Japan fortified these islands in violation of international treaties.
>
> The prosecution submitted reconnaissance photographs taken by American military aircraft immediately before the Pacific War. These pictures clearly indicated that the construction of military and naval bases had just begun. When I pointed out the fact on the basis of prosecution evidence, the indictment was squashed and photographs withdrawn.[34]

General Okumiya stated:

> The Imperial Navy's official records stated that the first naval outfit assigned to the mandated islands was the Fourth Fleet, which moved into its main anchorage at Truk, not Saipan, 10 December 1939. This was many days after World War II broke out in Europe. The League of Nations had lost its function by that time.[35]

Commander Hideo Sekino, now a military commentator, stated:

> I visited Jaluit, Truk and Saipan for the first time in 1929 as a member of the training cruise of midshipmen. In 1933, I, as an officer of the training squadron, revisited these islands and also Eniwetok. In both tours, I never met a single navy seaman or officer. I met only civilians and natives.[36]

Rear Admiral Adatoshi Tomioka, Chief of the Operations Division in the Navy, Chief of Staff at the end of the Pacific war, summed up the Navy's position when he stated:

> In the 1930s the Navy never obtained or tried to obtain the Imperial sanction for the fortification of the mandated area. Such an idea did not occur to us. Of course it was preposterous for the Navy to consider fortification without an Imperial sanction. Navy leaders knew too well what could have been the Emperor's reaction, even if we had dared to consider fortification.[37]

The rumors concerning stationing military aircraft in the mandate islands in violation of the treaties were also apparently unfounded. General Okumiya states:

> The first Japanese naval aircraft to fly to Saipan were two twin-engined, Type 15 flying boats which made the flight from Yokosuka in

February 1929 for training purposes. Thereafter, from time to time similar flights by seaplanes and flying boats of the Imperial Navy took place from seaplane tenders or ground bases to the mandated islands. The first carrier-based, single-engined Japanese plane flew to Saipan in 1933. And the first ground-based, twin-engined planes flew from Japan to the Marianas, Carolines, and Marshalls in the spring of 1941.[38]

If the Japanese Army, Navy and Air Forces did not station units in the mandated islands or fortify them, it is logical for us to look at what was done and by whom. According to an affidavit made by the late Haruji Matsue, the founder and president of the South Pacific Islands Agency (Nanyo Kohatsu) which governed and developed the mandated islands, his corporation was never assigned any military function, nor did it have any policing authority. The corporation's business included agriculture, phosphate mining, fishing, transportation, civil construction and financing. It did build harbors and other related structures, not military or naval bases.[39]

The League of Nations Mandates Commission, in questioning the Japanese representative during the 1930s, indicated that there was some doubt that all of the construction was for commercial purposes. If this accusation was not true, there is at least a possibility that some of the construction could have been for dual purposes, commercial and military. General Okumiya states that the Imperial Navy carried out various hydrographical surveys of the islands. Such investigations included a search in the 1920s for islets and atolls that could be used by submarines, and there were similar missions by the seaplane tender *Kamoi* in 1935, 1936 and 1937.[40]

Rear Admiral Kanae Kozaka, who commanded the *Kamoi* in 1937, stated:

> The objective of the survey was to find and appraise space in the island suitable for construction of air stations. I examined the drying yards made in 1933 at Saipan and in 1935 at Truk by Nanyo Kohatsu by expansion of sugar cane fields. I also found two or three lots of Peleiu of the Palau and other islands that could potentially be made into runways.[41]

Referring to the drying yards mentioned by Admiral Kozaka, Rear Admiral Kato stated:

> I served as chief of the administration section in charge of all Naval air station affairs at the Navy Air Administration Command for two years from 1936 to 1937. All through my tour of duty, I never took note of any naval air base or station in the mandated islands.

One of the documents available to me only stated that there were drying yards belonging to Nanyo Kohatsu in Saipan and Truk. The drying yards were for drying farm and marine products, but were obviously spacious enough for non-scheduled or forced landing by small aircraft. But there were no Naval or civilian establishments in either of these drying yards. Under any definition, I should not believe that it was warranted to classify them as aerodromes. I may add that some of my fellow officers thought it advisable to create a similar drying yard at Palau also.[42]

The Nanyo Corporation also constructed a seaplane base at Saipan in 1937, but claimed it was not for Navy aircraft. In fact, Japan Air Lines flew genuine commercial routes from Yokohama to Palau via Saipan commencing in 1939. Among the pilots were some reserve naval pilots.[43]

In summary, the Japanese writer, General Okumiya, destroyed the myth of prewar fortification of the mandated islands. However, the base structure of the Nanyo Corporation was easily converted to military use when the treaties had expired and war was imminent.

Based on the above information, it seems conclusive that the Japanese did not fortify the Pacific mandated islands in the classic, dictionary sense of building large and permanent strongholds in violation of the League of Nations Mandate and the status quo provisions of the Washington Naval Conference. Prior to the commencement of World War II in Europe, evidence indicates that they did not build concrete gun emplacements, hardened command and control centers, and other construction associated with "fortification." Additionally, no organized military units were permanently stationed in the mandated islands during the period in question.

On the other hand, there appears to have been considerable cooperation between the commercial construction programs of the Nanyo Corporation and the requirements of the Japanese military forces. These facilities provided the base structure for naval bases, fuel facilities, repair shops and airfields which were easily converted to military use when the requirement was generated in the late 1930s. Additionally, the many surveys made by the Japanese Navy and its air arm during the 1920s and 1930s made it possible for the military to launch almost immediately into required fortifications and building programs when the war was about to start.

In conclusion, it can be assumed that the original and subsequent charges of fortification were based on either misinformation, suspicion, or a lack of information. Further, it is believed that the major fortification charges were made at a time when, as a result of the Manchuria episode and other incidents in China, large sections of the western world were disposed to believe any charges against Japan. The mere possession of the islands by the Japanese caused the Navy grave concern. They believed war was approaching in the Pacific and the mandated islands provided not only refuges for submarines but scores of havens for naval aircraft. The fact that the fortification of these islands was a myth was fortunate for the United States. As a Marine, I wonder what the score card would show if the mandated islands had been fortified to the same degree as the Bonins.

8 / The Caroline Islands

Frederic L. Nystrom,

Commander, United States Navy

The Caroline Islands are a division of Micronesia consisting of many small volcanic and coral islands in the tropics of the North Pacific Ocean. The western-most islands of the group come within 500 miles of the Philippines and span eastward for almost two thousand miles to the Marshall Islands. In a north-south direction, they extend from the equator northward about 700 miles. Of the hundreds of islets and islands, there are five main clusters where the majority of the population and commercial centers are located: Yap, Truk, Ponape, Palau, and Kusaie. There are some fifty island groups in all, which cover nearly 500 square miles of land area encircled by about one and a half million square miles of ocean.

Though the islands are all basically volcanic in origin, there is a geo-logical distinction between the eastern and western Carolines. The western islands are more "youthful" in character and are not yet considered true atolls; whereas, the eastern islands have subsided to a sufficient degree so that they have fully developed, encircling coral reefs. Only Yap and Palau fall into the former category. The Palau Islands, the most important of the clusters commercially, have about 143 square miles of land area. Truk's atoll, an older island group, has a diameter of almost 140 miles containing twelve volcanic islands the land mass of which totals fifty square miles. There are more than eighty coral islets centering on a wide, deep lagoon, many of which are awash during high tide. Ponape is the largest island, covering about 145 square miles. The Kusaie cluster contains more than 40 square miles of land.

The eastern Carolines were discovered by Alvaro Saavedra who sailed into the lagoon at Truk in 1528. Later, Villalobos, Miquel López de Legazpi, and Pedro Fernandes de Quiros discovered other islands of the group. The islands were named in 1868 by the Spanish Admiral Lezcano in honor of King Charles II. Until 1899 Spain held a loose sovereignty over the islands, and German, British, and American traders and missionaries developed footholds during this time. At the close of the Spanish-American War, Spain sold the islands to Germany who exploited them commercially, but failed to develop or fortify them. In October 1914 the Japanese occupied the islands for the Allied Powers and, after the war, with the support of Great Britain, France, and Russia, the Japanese gained control in the form of a mandate under the League of Nations. This gave Japan authority over the chain of islands in the Pacific from which she had feared an attack. Though the terms of the mandate forbade fortifications of the islands, there were frequent rumors that Japan was violating that stipulation. However, these rumors have never been founded in fact. During the time Japan held the islands, the warplane realized its potential and the fact that Japan was located on the flanks of America's vital Pacific supply lines began to be a concern to her statesmen. During World War II the Caroline bases of the Japanese proved difficult targets to assault and many had to be bypassed.

At the end of the war the United States retained possession of the islands and placed them under the aegis of the United Nations as a trust territory. For the next fifteen years, the islands of the Pacific, for which the United States had fought so hard and which were so vital to her security, were left to languish in the tropical heat of the South Pacific.

The statutory maximum of funds that could be requested by the administration was $7.5 million and the most that Congress ever appropriated was slightly over $6 million. These appropriations were only enough to cover the administrative costs connected with overseeing the trust with little left over for the urgent social and economic needs which the United States had pledged to promote when it accepted the trusteeship.

The Carolines were divided into the four administrative districts of Palau, Yap, Truk, and Ponape; and then, except for essential medical, social and regulatory services, the natives were left to their own devices. In 1951 the administration of the Carolines was transferred from the Department of the Navy to the Department of the Interior. The Navy, however, retained security control to regulate visitors, and few were allowed. Despite civilian control, few changes in administration were apparent; that is, few changes until the early 1960s. At that time, the number of trust territories was steadily dwindling and the newly independent nations of the world, through the United Nations, began to press the United States concerning the lack of development of its trust and query when the islands would be ready for independence.

On 14 December 1960, following a historic debate, the United Nations General Assembly expressed its concern and desire for the speedy attainment of independence by the colonial countries in a resolution entitled: *Declaration on the Granting of Independence to Colonial Countries and Peoples*. At the 1147th meeting of the United Nations Trusteeship Council, on 13 June 1961, Mr. Jonathan Bingham, the United States Minister to the Council, stated that the United States Government considered the essential elements of the 1960 General Assembly Resolution applicable to the Trust Territory of the Pacific Islands. He went on to say that his government was taking continuing steps to stimulate the political development of the territory in the direction of increased self-government, with a view toward giving the people free choice with respect to their political future.[1]

Under the glaring spotlight of world opinion, the United States, through its High Commissioner of the trust territory, M. Wilfred Goding, instituted new concepts in the promotion of the welfare of the natives. The repatriation of the Japanese following World War II had left the islands without a trained administrative cadre and with virtually no commerce. The American policy had been to protect the natives from foreign commercial exploitation and preserve the limited natural resources for their exclusive use. Without the necessary skills available and with their lands ravaged by the recent war, the islanders were extremely slow to recover. None of the industries today have reached prewar status, but there has been rapid advancement in the past several years. The military restrictions have been relaxed or removed, travelers can get in and news concerning the area can get out. In 1961 the legal maximum for the budget was raised to $17.5 million; in 1967 it became $25 million; and for fiscal years 1968 and 1969, $35 million; and by 1972, $60 million.[2] Though the appropriations may not always coincide with the authorized maximum, progress has been made in more ample funds for the development of the political, social, economic, and educational training of the indigenous inhabitants has been assured.

The islands still lack the makings of a viable economy. Agriculture at a subsistance production-level is still the mainstay of life for the natives of the outlying islands as it has been for many years. No important mineral resources have been discovered since the location of extensive phosphate deposits on the islands of Angaur and Peleliu in the Palau group in 1903. The copra trade, the mainstay of the economy, suffered badly during World War II and is only now approaching prewar production standards. It is, however, the major export of the islands. The fishing industry was becoming highly developed under the Japanese administration, but it did not include the indigenous inhabitants. An extensive fisheries training program started recently in Palau is not showing signs of success because the natives, used to an easy life in the tropics, have shown little inclination towards the hard work involved. Plans are still progressing for other training programs in Truk and there is optimism that they will succeed. In conjunction with the fisheries training program at Palau, a small shipyard has been constructed and fishing boats as long as 75 feet have been built there. Repair facilities are also available.[3] To assist the small businessmen and traders, a number of cooperatives and credit unions have been established, and they have done an amazingly brisk and successful business. These are located primarily in the Palaus where a money economy has developed. The islands as a whole, however, suffer from a deficit economy and have consistently imported about twice as much as they export with local revenues falling further and further behind expenditures. The only way these deficits can be compensated for is by Congressional appropriations, a situation which in part explains the recent increases.

More than half of the population is under the age of twenty, a fact which places an extremely heavy burden on the limited educational facilities which are available. The degree of education of the indigenous inhabitants ranges from virtually none in the outlying islands, through the fourth or fifth grade in the middle-sized communities, and a complete high school education in the major population centers. A small number of students have continued their education at colleges and universities, primarily in Hawaii, most of them under grants from United Nations Fellowships or American government scholarships.

The school systems were previously financed exclusively by appropriations from the district legislatures (these appropriations have more than quadrupled since 1963), but they are now supplemented by funds made available through the federal government. The United States Elementary and Secondary School Act of 1965 made provisions for the furtherance of education in the trust territories and provided funds for additional elementary school teachers commencing with the fall of 1966.

Social advancement in the Carolines has been accelerated as well. Primarily the emphasis has been placed on improvement of the medical facilities and availability of skilled medical help, including the training of indigenous doctors at the medical school in Suva, Fiji Islands. Though their medical degrees are not recognized for practicing in the United States these doctors are highly skilled and are contributing a great deal to the advancement of public and individual health in their communities. Also, special emphasis has been placed on the educational and social advancement of women. In 1963 special training programs were conducted in these fields in collaboration with the East-West Center in Hawaii.

In the area of public works, many roads, airfields, sewage systems, and electric power plants have been repaired, refurbished, or revamped in the past six or seven years, many of which had been neglected since the end of World War II. Surface transportation has been improved by the chartering of three inter-island steamers from a New York firm, which in turn has formed a corporation in the islands and is using native labor for crews, including seventeen ship's officers. Air transportation had previously been provided by the Trust Territory Commission. Now, however, it is being taken over by Continental Airlines which will provide scheduled jet air service between Guam and six key Micronesian islands including three in the Carolines. From Guam, passengers will be able to connect with air service to all major cities in the world. The Caroline Islands which will benefit from this new service are: Truk, Palau, and Ponape. All of the airfields are now ready for this service with the exception of Ponape which is in the process of construction. Rapid transportation will not be the only benefit derived from this arrangement, for the contract also calls for Continental to build a twenty-five unit motel within the next three years at each of the points served. Thus, adequate facilities for tourists have been provided in the islands for the first time in history. This step was heralded by a high federal official in Washington as the first real step in the development of Micronesia.[4]

Starting in 1964 the Peace Corps expanded its operations into the trust territory with plans to eventually have workers spread throughout the islands providing assistance in the form of: elementary and secondary school teachers, experienced Peace Corps community development workers, health aids, nurses, pharmacists, laboratory technicans, x-ray technicians, civil engineers, surveyors, architects and planners, lawyers and small business advisors. Their aim is to teach the natives the skills necessary to develop a self-sufficient territory. There is a second phase of Peace Corps activities planned which will bring skills in the areas of agriculture, credit union and cooperative development, additional teachers and public health volunteers and broadcasting and communications workers. All of these activities will be carried out in the more remote areas of the territory and are designed to supplement, not replace, the other American workers already in the islands.[5]

The people of the Carolines have come a long way in the past six or seven years, but are they ready for independence of the type envisioned by the United Nations? It is at least questionable whether they are ready now, or if they will ever be capable of complete independence. Even if they should in some way overcome the barriers of several diverse languages, caste systems, and the vast stretches of water which geographically separate them, the natives of the Carolines do not have the resources available to become economically independent. Three alternate courses of action are available if the trusteeship must be terminated:

1. They could become a formal territory of the United States similar to the Virgin Islands and Puerto Rico.

2. They could become a state of the United States, or part of one of the other states. Hawaii has suggested this alternative.

3. They could become a territory or a part of another country.

All of these possibilities have a certain degree of merit, or at least plausibility. On 21 August 1967 President Lyndon B. Johnson requested the Congress to establish a commission to consider the future status of the Trust Territory of the Pacific Islands and to study the desirability of calling a plebiscite before 30 June 1972 to permit the Micronesians to decide their governmental future.[6] The commission, after several months delay, has now been established, and the general consensus of opinion is that the plebiscite will be held no earlier than 1972. The Presidential request was in response to a Joint House-Senate Resolution introduced by Senator Mike Mansfield and Representative Jonathan Bingham (D-N.Y.), (previously the United States delegate on the United Nations Trusteeship Council). In his introduction, Senator Mansfield stated that the United States had failed in its obligations to the people of the trust territory and the United Nations. He went on to say that there were many who contend that life for the islanders was better under the Japanese, who at least had a commercial interest in the area and therefore began developing by providing roads, a water supply, electric power and schools. The Senator castigated the administrations, past and present, for not requesting sufficient funds to do justice to the islanders.

After President Johnson's request for a study of the situation, several Americans visited the islands and interviewed a sampling of the natives in order to determine a concensus of their opinion. The general trend of the answers was that none of the islanders felt that they would be ready for independence at the time of the plebiscite, or that they would even be ready to determine what their future desires would be. The opinion was advanced that the majority of the young persons would be in favor of continued association with the United States in some manner, but that many of the older natives would favor the resumption of Japanese rule. The Japanese influence is returning to the islands. Early in 1946 the Japanese were granted permission to resume mining the phosphate rock at Angaur, but only under strictly controlled conditions. Until 1962 they, and most other persons (including Americans), were virtually excluded from visiting the Carolines. At that time the islands were opened to visitors though few immediately took advantage of it. Now Japanese merchants are resuming their trade in the islands and the natives prefer many of the Japanese manufactured goods, though it is primarily because they are cheaper. In May 1967 direct air service was inaugurated between Guam and Tokyo. This has caused a large influx of Japanese tourists into Guam and many continue into the trust territory. By November the monthly average of Japanese tourists arriving on Guam had climbed to 700 with all indications pointing toward a continued increase. When jet service into the island groups is effected, there is not much doubt that Japanese tourists in the trust territory will show a further increase.[7]

Through the relatively short period of their known history, the Caroline Islands have run the gamut from being considered so insignificant that they were completely ignored to a period in which they were so vitally important to so many nations of the world that great battles were fought on their shores and thousands of men died in the struggle for their control. In the early years, Spain loosely maintained a discoverer's claim to the islands. She rose from lethargy only when her suzerainty was challenged, and once again assigned them to oblivion. When her Pacific empire crumbled, Spain sold the islands to the highest bidder, Germany. Though she exploited the islands commercially, she ignored their strategic importance as an outpost from which she could control the Pacific and failed to fortify them against attack.

The United States, though involved in China from the mid-nineteenth century and as a landlord of Pacific Island outposts since 1898, failed to recognize the importance of the 2,000-mile-long flank to her vital supply lines until it was too late. This is unfortunate because she had several opportunities to acquire all or a portion of the islands in the preceding sixty years. When Japan decided to occupy the islands in 1914, American statesmen at last came to the realization that foreign control of these tiny specks of coral and volcanic rock could pose a threat to the Philippines and Guam.

Japanese military men won their government's support for continuing to occupy the former German island-colonies with the argument that only by control of the Pacific Island chains could Japan preclude the threat of a dagger pointed directly at their southern shores. In public statements, the Japanese admirals contended that their control of the former German colonies was necessary for their defense, but that Japanese control did not present a threat to any other nation because of the great distances involved. During the short span of Japanese occupation of the Carolines, however, the potential of the airplane was realized and the purported cushion of the vast expanse of ocean disappeared as far as the United States was concerned. The juxtaposition of the Japanese islands to Hawaii, then the United States's keystone of the Pacific, began to concern the American military strategists so much that they suspected that the attack on Pearl Harbor would come from the mandated islands.

After the agonizing process of island-hopping two-thirds of the way across the Pacific, the United States was determined to retain possession of these islands which had held such a strategic position during World War II. The presumption of the insulation and protection provided by the vast expanse of the Pacific which prevailed prior to World War II, changed at the end of that conflict. The popular concept of American naval strategy came to be reckoned by the number of forward bases instead of the number of battleships. Americans developed the ambivalent feeling that the Pacific was both narrow enough for the United States to control and wide enough to provide her shelter. It was, in the words of General Douglas MacArthur, "a vast moat to protect us as long as we hold it."

In the 1950s the popular conception of any future war was that it would be global, swift, and nuclear. Events since that time have proven such a hypothesis to be incorrect. The strategic value of the Carolines, so highly prized in war and so quickly forgotten in peace, remains today fully as important as it was twenty-five years ago. At the present time, they provide a potential second line of defense.

As such, it is vitally important that the United States retain its influence. To succeed in this, the United States must develop these tiny pieces of rock and coral to their full economic potential and continue to cultivate the friendship of the indigenous inhabitants—in other words, to meet the obligations of international trusteeship.

9 / The Mariana Islands

John R. Lincoln,

Commander, United States Navy

Extending southward from Japan is a submerged volcanic ridge that stretches to New Guinea. The exposed peaks of this ridge include the Mariana Islands, which lie within the tropics between 13° and 20° north latitude. There are 183 square miles of land area in the 14 single islands and one group of three small islands north of Guam. Guam has 225 square miles, or more than the combined total of the other islands of the Marianas. The total land area of all the Marianas amounts to only about one-third the area of even our smallest state, Rhode Island.

The Marianas north of Guam currently make up the Marianas District of the Trust Territory of the United States. Under the Japanese, this same area was referred to as the "Saipan Administrative Section." In this discussion the islands north of Guam will be referred to as the "Marianas District."

Studies of the Marianas, including a site study on Saipan, established that man had arrived in this part of the Marianas by 1500 B.C. Undoubtedly the original settlers in the Marianas migrated from the Malaysian area.[1] The native people of the Marianas, known as Chamorros, resemble Filipinos and Asians, generally. Their customs, language, food, and culture have been modified over the last 400 years until the "pure Chamorro" no longer exists. The cultural heritage of the present-day people of the Marianas includes Spanish, Italian, French, English, Scotch, German, Japanese, Chinese, Mexican, Filipino, and American.[2]

Magellan, sailing in the service of Spain, landed on Guam in the

Marianas on 6 March 1521 at Umatic Bay. Magellan bestowed the name of Islas de Velas Latinas on these islands, but quickly re-christened them Islas de los Ladrones (Islands of Thieves) because he considered the natives to be shameless thieves.[3]

The first Spaniards to reside permanently in the Marianas arrived in 1668. The name Mariana comes from the patroness of these first settlers, Queen Maria Ana de Austria.[4] From 1521 until 1898 the Marianas were under Spanish rule. Guam became the center of Spanish life and commerce in general in the area.

An attempt was made by Americans to set up a colony on Agrihan Island in the Marianas early in the 19th century.

> In 1810, Captain Brown and other Americans, with several families of Hawaiians, formed a colony on this island (Agrihan), but it was broken up by the Spaniards, who destroyed the plantations.[5]

On 22 June 1898 the island of Guahan (Guam) was taken from the Spanish by the cruiser *Charleston* and American sovereignty in the Ladrones was declared.[6] The Marianas, less Guam, and the Carolines were sold by Spain to Germany in February 1899 for a sum of $4 million.[7] This was the beginning of the separation of one of the Marianas from the remainder of the group that continues to this day.

Germany took possession of the northern Marianas, in addition to the Carolines, on 1 October 1899. Saipan was the seat of administration for the German Marianas, but after a few years it lapsed into such unimportance that the German administrator moved to Yap and visited the Marianas only occasionally. The Marianas were the least productive of any island group in their protectorate and in the end, proved to be a financial burden to the German administration.[8]

German rule in the Marianas, as well as in other islands under their control north of the equator in the Pacific, ended in October 1914 when Japan seized the islands. The Treaty of Versailles, signed 28 June 1919, conferred a mandate on Japan including these islands. This mandate was confirmed in December 1920, and the United States gave its consent to this arrangement in a treaty with Japan signed 11 February 1922.[9]

The strategic importance of these islands to the Japanese is illustrated in the following statement:

> In the eyes of Japanese statesmen and naval experts, their country's long sought primacy in the Far East depended in no small degree on permanent occupation of the Marianas, Carolines, and Marshall archipelagoes seized from Germany in the early weeks of the World War [I].[10]

The period under the Japanese Mandate saw a large influx of Japanese, Koreans, and Okinawans to engage in agricultural activities, for the most part. The number of Japanese in the Saipan Administrative Section (the same area that is now included in the Marianas District) increased from 80 during the German administration in the early 20th century to 1,758 in 1920 and to 42,688 in 1937. This increase was from approximately 2% to 34% to 91% of the total population in the section for these years respectively.[11]

The agricultural development of the mandate was centered chiefly in the Saipan Administrative Section. Under the mandate the sugar plantations of Saipan, Tinian, and Rota became by far the largest enterprise in the area.

The dimension of tremendous economic development in the agricultural sector fostered by the Japanese is evident when one looks at the sugar industry. In 1916 there were 20 hectares (a hectare is about 2½ acres) in sugar cane. This increased to 459 hectares by 1919, 3,226 hectares in 1927 and 6,586 hectares in 1932.[12]

The civilian population, other than the Chamorros who only leased land to the Japanese, was almost exclusively engaged in the sugar industry. Copra was about the only agricultural industry that remained in the hands of the Chamorros. However, copra accounted for only one half of one percent, by value, of the agricultural production in the Marianas and only four percent of all copra production in the mandated territory.[13]

Agricultural products in the Saipan Administrative Section in 1938 included sugar, copra, rice, pineapple, cotton, corn, coffee, tobacco, oranges, bananas, tangerines, potatoes and tapioca.[14] Commercial fishing was the second most important enterprise under the Japanese administration and was centered in Saipan. It was scientifically organized and between 1930 and 1940 the tuna catch in the Saipan Administrative Section increased from just over a half million pounds to over seven million pounds per year.[15]

A feeling for the difference in the economy of the mandated Marianas, when compared to Guam, under United States administration, can be seen in the following statement by an executive in the Japanese sugar industry:

> A pity! The largest and most fertile of all these islands, and not used. While Guam's exports have been about $100,000 annually, those of Saipan, half its size, have been, under Japanese management, four times as much.[16]

Under the Japanese, the Marianas were transformed from the liability that they had been under German administration to "the richest asset of

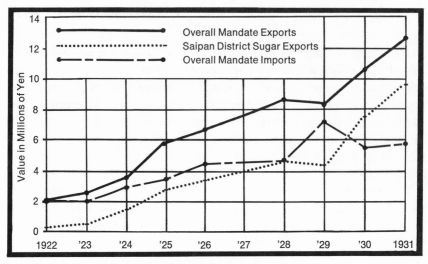

Imports versus Exports during Japanese
Administration of the Mandate

[R. W. Robson, The Pacific Islands Year Book, 4th ed. (Sydney: Pacific
Publications Pty. Ltd. 1942) p. 95]

all the Micronesian Islands."[17] The mandated islands under the Japanese
had a economy heavily balanced in her favor if one compares the exports
to imports. In 1931, for example, the value of exports was 214% of imports
for the mandate. Sugar and alcohol alone from the Saipan Administrative
Section accounted for 75% of the exports of the mandate. This gives some
feeling for the agricultural potential of the Marianas, and is illustrated in
Figure 1. Note in Figure 1 that after 1929 the exports from the Saipan
Administrative Section more than balanced the imports to the entire
Japanese mandate.

Japan continued to administer the mandate even after withdrawal from
the League of Nations. The controversy as to whether these islands were
fortified by the Japanese before World War II continues today. It seems
likely that military fortifications in the strictest sense probably did not
start until just prior to the outbreak of World War II.[18]

At about 8:30 a.m. on 8 December 1941 the first Japanese bombs carried
by nine Saipan-based planes fell on Guam. This act ushered the Marianas
into World War II.

On 22 February 1944 United States naval aircraft from Task Force 58,
a fast carrier task force, attacked the Marianas for the first time in World
War II.[19] D-Day for Saipan was 15 June 1944, when American forces
landed and bitter fighting with heavy losses on both the American side

and the Japanese side occurred. Later in June Tinian was invaded and in July of 1944 Guam was invaded by American forces.

The loss of Saipan shook the Japanese government to its roots. For Japan, this meant that once American bombers were established in the Marianas, Tokyo was within their range. Almost immediately after the shocking news of the loss of Saipan reached Tokyo, Premier Tojo was relieved as head of the Japanese Army and on 18 July 1944 the Tojo cabinet fell.[20]

The islands of the Marianas, other than Saipan, Tinian and Guam, were neutralized by aerial and naval gunfire and bypassed. The surrender of the Japanese on some of the islands of the Marianas was not effected until September 1945. With the seizure of the Marianas by the U.S. from the Japanese in World War II, the islands passed into the hands of the fourth great power to administer them in less than fifty years.

The U.S. Navy was in control of the former Japanese mandate at the end of hostilities in the Pacific. However, the matter of control and administration, as well as the political future of the Pacific Islands, was to be wrangled over for many months.

President Truman temporarily approved the naval administration of the former mandated islands in September 1945. The following month a committee made up of the Secretaries of State, War, Navy, and Interior was appointed to make a recommendation as to the administration of the former mandated islands. The strategic security aspect of the islands was uppermost in these discussions over the islands. The initial discussions continued for over a year and there developed two sides to the basic issue of method of control.[21]

On the one side was the defense establishment, which favored full United States sovereignty of the islands through annexation. This approach would ensure the unrestricted use of these islands as major air and naval bases.

On the other side of the future status question were those who preferred trusteeship and "limiting the American bases to the minimum regarded as absolutely essential to American security and to the fulfillment of such international obligations as may fall to the lot of the United States."[22] Departments of State and Interior took this stand in general. This controversy over who should administer the former Japanese mandate developed into a campaign between Secretary of the Interior Harold L. Ickes and Secretary of the Navy James V. Forrestal that raged through the summer and fall of 1946. In a series of letters appearing in *The New York*

Times, during August and September of 1946, Ickes and Forrestal traded verbal salvos.[23] The Navy won out, at least temporarily, in the discussion of military versus civil administration in the Pacific Islands.

President Truman announced on 6 November 1946 that the United States was prepared to place the former Japanese mandated islands under United Nations trusteeship with the United States as administering authority. The trusteeship agreement was approved unanimously by the Security Council on 2 April 1947.[24] After Congressional authorization, the President approved the trusteeship agreement and it was made effective 18 July 1947.[25]

The trusteeship was, and is, unique in that the area of the Trust Territory of the Pacific Islands was designated a "strategic area." This was in accordance with Article 83 of the Charter of the United Nations. Article 5 of the trusteeship agreement authorizes the United States to "establish naval, military, and air bases and to erect fortifications in the trust territory, among other things."[26]

Military government in the former mandated islands ended on 18 July 1947 by Presidential order, and the Department of the Navy assumed responsibility for administration of the trust territory.

The Saipan District of the trust territory encompassed what today is included in the Marianas District; i.e., the Mariana Islands north of Guam. The Saipan District was administered by the Governor of the Northern Marianas. Additionally, there was a Civil Administrator Saipan who was also the Commanding Officer, Naval Personnel, Civil Administration Unit. By 1950 military and naval activities had decreased in the northern Marianas, in general, and Saipan, in particular, and the title of governor ceased to exist. The Civil Administrator for the Saipan District handled all administrative functions in the district for the remainder of the naval administration.

For most of the time of naval administration there was a naval administrator on Tinian. On Rota, except for short periods when there was a resident administrator, the natives ran the island themselves. During this period (from 1947 until 1951) Alamagan, Agrihan, and Pagan, as well as Rota, were serviced by field trips from the District Administration on Saipan.

While the northern Marianas were administered as a portion of the trust territory, Guam resumed the status of a territory of the United States after liberation from the Japanese. In 1946 the military government ended and naval government was reestablished. In 1950 an Organic Act was passed by the United States Congress. This act not only conferred American citizenship on Guamanians, but allowed a civil administration with a limited amount of self government. Thus ended a period of military and naval rule for Guam of some 300 years under both the Spanish and Americans, not to mention the three years under the Japanese.

One problem that developed right after the war was that of the U.S. Government's use of land for military installations. In the years immediately following the war virtually the entire island of Saipan was used by the military. On Guam about 42% of the land was owned or controlled by the government. The extensive military bases, especially on Saipan and Guam, provided employment for large numbers of the Chamorros.

The problem of land usage in the Marianas was complicated by the existence of unexploded ordnance, especially on Rota and Saipan. Although the problem on Rota, and to a lesser extent on Saipan, was reduced, a large section of northern Saipan is fenced off and out-of-bounds.

Attempts during the naval administration to establish commercial scale farms on Saipan, and especially Tinian, were of limited success. The main problem was lack of *dependable* transportation to the markets on Guam. The Navy imported some livestock to Saipan and some small-scale ranching was carried out on Tinian and Rota. However, the raising of livestock was carried out only on a small scale by the end of the naval administration. Also, there were attempts to re-establish the commercial fishing industry, but this, too, met with limited success.

Naval administration, which in practice had been in effect since the northern Marianas had been taken from the Japanese, continued until 1 July 1951. In the period of the late 1940s and early 1950s various drafts of organic acts were submitted to Congress setting forth charters for governing the trust territory. Finally, without waiting for Congressional decision, the Executive branch directed the transfer of the trust territory from the Navy Department to the Interior Department. Thus, the campaign started at the end of World War II by Secretary Ickes ended with this transfer.

The administration of the Marianas District as a complete unit by the Department of the Interior continued for just eighteen months. Saipan and Tinian in the northern Marianas were declared military districts on 1 January 1953, when their administration was transferred from the Department of the Interior back to the Department of the Navy.[27]

On 17 July 1953 the responsibility for the civil administration of the remaining islands of the northern Marianas, with the exception of Rota, was transferred to the Secretary of the Navy.[28] This left the small island of Rota in "artificial political isolation,"[29] under the Department of the Interior. In 1955 Rota was made a separate district.[30] The people of Rota petitioned the United Nations for a reunion of the Marianas under one department or another, but their efforts were in vain. Seven years were to pass before their desire was fulfilled.[31]

This split of the Marianas District into the Saipan District and the Rota District "for special security purposes"[32] is rather nebulously referred to in many of the official documents with little mention of the actual use of the Saipan District[33] during the period 1953 to 1962. However, some of the references available provide interesting, if brief, comments concerning this period. During this period the United States Central Intelligence Agency had an installation on Saipan that was reported to have cost "some twenty-eight million dollars."[34]

On 1 July 1962 the headquarters for the entire trust territory was transferred from Guam to Saipan, where it occupied the buildings previously occupied by the Central Intelligence Agency. Simultaneously, the former Rota and Saipan Districts were amalgamated into the Mariana Islands District and administration reverted to the Department of the Interior.

A new charter for the Mariana Islands District Legislature was adopted on 21 December 1962. The charter provides for a unicameral body of sixteen representatives to be chosen every three years by the electors of the Marianas District of the trust territory.

The territory-wide Congress of Micronesia has only limited legislative powers. The United States Congress controls the budget for the trust territory. The Congress of Micronesia may pass laws, but the High Commissioner has veto power. Allowance has been made so that should the occasion arise where a law passed by the Congress of Micronesia is vetoed twice the legislators may appeal to the Secretary of the Interior.

The keen interest in government affairs shown by the citizens of the Marianas District is illustrated by the voter participation in 1966 when over 98% of the eligible voters went to the polls.[35] Some of the reasons that probably account for these high figures when compared to the other districts are: better transportation, better communications, common language, organized political party system and, generally, more "westernized" attitude to government participation.

Today's economy in the Marianas District of the trust territory is based primarily upon subsistence farming and, to a lesser extent, fishing. Primary exports from the Marianas District are copra, livestock, fruit, vegetables,

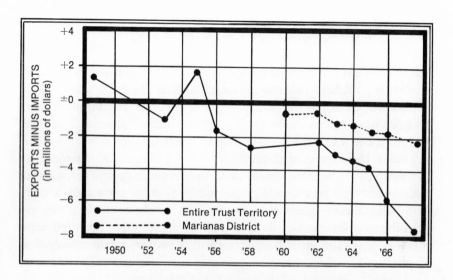

Balance of Trade for the Trust Territory
and the Marianas District

and fish. Further, there are no forests of commercial value, no known mineral resources, no major manufacturing activities nor large commercial ventures in the district.[36] To the resources can be added scrap metal from World War II battlegrounds, a rapidly diminishing source of income.

An interesting comparison of the Japanese mandate to the current trust territory is shown in the following statement:

> Economic well-being of the region is far less than it was during the Japanese occupation of the area before the war. The U.S. has done little to encourage local development. The natives have done less.[37]

In contrast to the positive "balance of trade" during the period of the Japanese mandate, the imports exceeded the exports in the Marianas District by over 750% in fiscal year 1967.[38]

The *potential* for agriculture in the Marianas District is by far the greatest of any district in the trust territory. Fifty-three percent of the land in the Marianas District is considered arable, with another fifteen percent usable as grazing land. However, almost eighty-six percent of the arable land in the Marianas District is not being used.[39] This large amount of unused arable land is partially because of the scattered live ammunition over many acres of Saipan. An even more important reason seems to be a general lack of interest in farming by a large portion of the population.

Fresh vegetables and fruits are exported mostly by air to Guam, where the Defense Department installations provide a good market for produce.

Because of various insect problems, such as the fruit fly, these products are closely monitored and, at times, excluded from Guam.

Each district of the trust territory has at least one experimental project that has economic merit. In the Marianas, where there is relatively good pasturage, beef cattle thrive especially on Tinian.

Tourist trade could well provide a large portion of the income for Micronesia. A factor that should help spur economic growth is the recent inauguration of thrice-weekly, island-to-island jet air service for six key islands in the territory, including Saipan.

In the area of trade, one thing that has held back exports to the United States is the continued import duty on trust territory goods. The *Nathan Plan* summarizes this problem as follows:

> While a more liberal United States tariff policy is not a guarantee that offshore commercial fishing [or other commercial enterprises] will be an important industry in the trust territory, a continuation of the present United States tariff restrictions will virtually assure that the industry will never be more than marginal.[40]

The two major trade centers for Micronesia are the United States and Japan. The trust territory exported goods amounting to $160,000 to the United States, whereas Japan's share was worth $3,000,000 in 1965. On the other hand, imports from Japan were only $2,000,000 compared to $4,500,000 from the United States for the same year.[41] However, distances must be considered. It is over 5,000 nautical miles from Saipan to San Francisco and only about 1,300 nautical miles from Saipan to Tokyo. It seems likely that even closer economic ties to Japan are probable in the future.

President Johnson, on 21 August 1967, asked Congress to establish a commission to consider the future status of the Trust Territory of the Pacific Islands. This commission is to study the desirability of calling a plebiscite before 1972 to permit the people of the trust territory to voice their desire as to what their governmental future should be.[42]

There has been at least one attempt in the Marianas District to obtain a "grass roots" feeling for the desires of the islanders. A plebiscite was held on Saipan in 1961[43] and out of a total of 2,847 registered voters, 2,517 voted to become citizens of the United States, either through unification with Guam or as a separate territory, and only 27 indicated a preference for the *status quo*.[44]

The possibility of the detachment of Saipan or the Marianas from the trust territory and unification with nearby Guam is opposed by some

Guamanians because of potential economic competition as well as suspicions stemming from World War II. The military support of the
Japanese given by some Saipanese is resented on pro-American Guam and
might cause political tension in the event of union.[45]

There was a United Nations Visiting Mission in 1964 that considered
the political future of the trust territory. They considered two alternatives—full independence or some form of integration with the United
States. Independence would mean Micronesia's standing on its own
strength with a cessation of United States aid. Their conclusions were
that:

> . . . since Micronesia is clearly not self-sufficient . . . the only alterna-
> tive was some form of integration with the United States, either as
> part of Hawaii or part of the Territory of Guam.[46]

If the strategic value of the Marianas to the United States was doubted
in 1898, 1914 or 1922, it was made clear when Saipan-based Japanese
planes bombed Guam on 8 December 1941.[47] The heavy toll in American
lives and material expended in 1944 in the seizure of the Marianas made
the strategic value of these islands painfully evident to Washington.

In more recent years, these islands are especially important not only
from a missile and nuclear war viewpoint, but they have great potential
value as bases in a limited war. Additionally, these islands have value as
weather stations, launching or tracking stations for missiles and space satel-
lites and as bases from which to monitor the movement of hostile submarines.[48]

A recent article describes how strategists in Washington are looking
ahead to the day when United States bases in Japan, Okinawa, and the
Philippines might be relinquished. Experts estimated in 1967 that this
could happen in from three to five years and currently negotiations are in
progress to reduce the United States presence in Japan and Japan will
assume an ever increasing defense role in Okinawa and the rest of the
Ruyukus. One possible answer to the question of where to move these
bases is:

> The preference of top military planners is already known. There
> will be a withdrawal to the Mariana Islands, if present planning is
> approved.[49]

This article indicated that a survey of the installation at Guam revealed the
island was not nearly large enough for future needs, since it is about 35

miles long and 4 to 8 miles wide. Further, it stated that: "Military officials would like to fortify four separate islands in the Marianas."[50] These officials, aware of the problems likely to be encountered with the U.S. State Department as well as the United Nations, ". . . insist it is in America's vital interest to make the move despite the political consequences."[51]

The islands specifically mentioned as potential military bases in addition to Guam, are Rota, Tinian, and Saipan. Uses for the possible fortifications include major military headquarters, major bomber bases, deep-water fleet anchorage, atomic stockpiling, troop staging, missile bases, advanced troop training and other military activities.

Legally there is nothing to stop our fortifying these islands. Article 5, paragraph 1 of the *Trusteeship Agreement for the Former Japanese Mandated Islands* specifically authorizes the administering authority to ". . . establish naval, military, and air bases and to erect fortifications in the trust territory. . . ."[52]

Hanson W. Baldwin, Military Editor of *The New York Times* for the past four decades, recently wrote: ". . . if the United States power is to be projected to the Pacific coast of Asia, the island bases in the Western Pacific must be retained, improved and made secure. . . ."[53] Further, Mr. Baldwin states that the bases of the Western Pacific, including Guam, cannot be ". . . permitted to fall into the hands of a potential enemy, *lest the security of the others be breached.*"[54]

Other writers have voiced the opinion that the return of the Bonins and Volcano Islands to Japan recently is the precursor to a shift in United States strategic defenses in the Pacific. One such comment was: ". . . the U.S. seemed to many to be taking the first long step toward a pullback to the Mariana Islands."[55]

As to the political future of the Trust Territory of the Pacific Islands, including the Marianas District, there is some disagreement as to whether the Micronesians should be offered the proposed plebiscite. Representative Patsy T. Mink recently stated in an address to the U.S. House of Representatives that it would be a "serious error to proceed with the resolution [calling for a plebiscite by 30 June 1972]. . . ."[56] In spite of Mrs. Mink's misgivings, she recently stated that:

> It does appear likely that the resolution calling for a plebiscite will pass the Congress. I do not favor it and have sponsored my own bill [H.R. 16183 introduced on 25 March 1968] providing for an Organic Act for the Trust Territory. . . .[57]

More specifically, concerning the Marianas, Representative Mink stated:

> Assuming the plebiscite returns are favorable to a closer relationship with the U.S., then I think it will be quite possible for the Marianas District to become consolidated with the Territory of Guam if that is the wish of the people of the Marianas. I believe that the Congress and the U.N. will be amenable to this move.[58]

From the above comments by Representative Mink, it would appear that a plebiscite will probably be held in the trust territory within a few years. If alternatives are offered the Micronesians, and the plebiscite includes allowances for individual districts to select different courses of action, it is possible that the citizens of the Marianas could opt for reunification (for the first time in over 50 years) of all the Mariana Islands. This *could* separate the Marianas District from the remainder of the trust territory. It is interesting that Representative Mink feels that the Congress and the United Nations would most likely agree to such an arrangement. If this possible course of action is offered the Mariana islanders, then the desires of the Guamanians would have to be obtained also.

The possibility has been suggested that, should the Congress of the United States fail to provide for a viable political future for Micronesia "through neglect, cultural arrogance or careless indifference, we will have exposed our Achilles Heel to the shafts of Communist adventurism."[59]

The political future of the Marianas District, as well as the entire trust territory, is tied to, not only the actions of the U.S. Congress and U.S. strategic policy, but to the islanders' own economic viability. Dr. Elbert V. Bowden, economic analyst of Robert R. Nathan Associates, commented that: "Micronesia will never have a viable economy without heavy injections of capital, management and labor."[60]

Resolving the political question by granting independence, territorial status, or keeping the status quo is not necessarily going to resolve the other problems which are economically oriented. Without a viable economic base on which to build, independence would not be a practical alternative. Status quo would keep the United Nations forum available to the islanders as a method of voicing any grievances against the United States administration. Territorial status would open some new avenues to help solve economic problems, such as special reductions or elimination of tariffs.

On the other hand, a balanced economy where exports exceed imports, improved health and living conditions, and a high standard of education does not necessarily mean that the political problems will be automatically solved. It *does* mean that there is a base on which to build a more sound political status, whether it be as a territory, an independent state, or a continuance of the trust territory status. It does appear that some political restlessness may be developing in the territory.

The Marianas District legislature, somewhat uncertain of their political future, recently passed separate resolutions "inviting aid from the Soviet Union and simultaneously asking Washington for a return of U.S. military bases, which had proved an unwonted windfall for the islands' economies during [and shortly following] World War II."[61]

It seems likely that a plebiscite will result in some form of association of Micronesia with the United States based on free will, probably similar to the commonwealth status of Puerto Rico. However, it is possible that the people of Micronesia *could* opt for independence. With the strategic importance of these islands to the United States, this could prove most embarrassing to the United States government.

The strategic importance of the Marianas is not likely to decrease in the foreseeable future and, if anything, could well increase. This would especially be true if the political climate become such in Japan, Okinawa, Taiwan, and the Philippines that United States base rights are curtailed or rescinded. In this case, the strategic importance of the trust territory, in general, and the Marianas Islands, in particular, would assume a strategic prominence of great proportions.

Any change in status or type of governmental administration that provides for more local autonomy, whether it be through more self-government or independence, must allow for and encourage more self-dependence. This seems possible only through a more viable economy. It seems likely that trade and contacts with Japan will increase in the future—to the mutual benefit of all concerned.

When comparing the Marianas District to the other districts of the Trust Territory of the Pacific Islands, it can be seen that the Marianas probably have the greatest potential, economically, politically, and strategically. Some reasons for this are a relatively larger land area, common language, a more developed political system, and strategic location in the central western Pacific Ocean. Specifically, the Marianas have potential for agricultural and tourist development, as well as for strategic military bases. It needs stimulation and help from outside the district and territory as well as ambition on the part of local people to want to improve their lot. Planning by the United States Congress as well as within the Marianas will be necessary to bring this area to its full potential.

10 / The Marshall Islands

C. W. Hunter,

Colonel, United States Marine Corps

The Marshall Islands have been referred to as being at the ends of the earth and, regardless of the motivation for such a remark, it is true. Marshallese are the first to see each day begin and last to see it end. Each day begins at the 180th meridian, the Marshalls lie just to the west of it between 160° 50′ and 172° 10′ east longitude. They are also near the lateral center of the earth lying between 40° 30′ and 14° 45′ north latitude.

The Marshall Islands are arranged roughly in two low-lying chains running from north-northwest to south-southeast. The easternmost row is called the Ratak ("sunrise" or "towards the dawn") Chain, comprised by fourteen atolls and two single islands. The western-most row called the Ralik ("sunset" or "towards the sunset" Chain, comprised by fifteen atolls and three single islands. Two of the Ralik northern atolls, Eniwetok and Ujelang, lie somewhat out of the general line of the other islands to the westward.

These two chains lie about 130 miles to 160 miles apart. Atolls lie an average of fifty miles apart in the same chain. The greatest distance between atolls is the 165 miles between Eniwetok and Bikini. Some are less than two miles apart, as in the case of Knox and Mille. All of the northern islands lie in the westward-running North Equatorial Current. Those islands in the southern region stand with the Equatorial countercurrent flowing eastward around them, at least from September to February. The total sea area of the Marshall Islands is about one and a half times the size of Texas or roughly 375,000 square miles. The total land area is about seventy square miles.

The tropical marine climate of the Marshalls, a consequence of their position in the low latitudes, provides a high and remarkably unchanging temperature which deviates no more than one degree in any month from an annual mean of 81°F. Humidity is very high and also shows only slight seasonal change—the daily mean being 83 to 84 percent. Heavy precipitation is common in the Marshalls, but its fall differs widely between localities and even in the same locality from time to time. Because the rainfall in the southern islands is most consistent, those islands are most heavily populated. In the northern islands they have occasional droughts, an occurrance which requires cooking in salt water from the lagoon and drinking coconut water and juice. However, in a drought, coconut trees are the first to die. Breadfruit, bananas, and taro can survive much better in the sandy dry soil.

Typhoons, bringing massive destruction to crops, trees and readily available food supplies are the most destructive natural hazards. They are almost always followed by famine and starvation when outside assistance is not provided.

All atolls and single islands in the Marshalls are formed exclusively of coral, and were built upward from submerged mountain peaks, which sometime in the ancient past rose close to the ocean's surface.

The constituent islands of an atoll, separated from one another by reefs and passages, vary in size from a few square yards to several square miles. Generally, they are long, narrow, and curved in conformity with the shape of the atoll. The longest islet is Majuro, of the atoll by the same name, which is nearly twenty-five miles long but only a few hundred yards wide. It is characteristic to find the higher and wider islets on the windward east side of all atolls in the Marshalls. The coral polyps receive more food there because the wind piles the ocean waters up there allowing them to build faster.[1]

Once-rare nocturnal predators, the "crown-of-thorns", seldom seen over a decade ago have undergone a mysterious population explosion and now feed upon coral reefs in widely scattered areas of the Pacific. The "crown-of-thorns" or *Acanthaster planci* is a starfish which extends its membranous stomach through its mouth and spreads it over the coral tissue. Digestive juices pour from the stomach membrane out over the coral to liquefy the polyps into a greenish slime. When the "crown-of-thorns" moves on, only skeleton coral remains. Investigations disclose that one "crown-of-thorns" can destroy (graze-out) an area twice the size of its six- to twelve-inch central disk in a single day. To date, this coral killer has killed ninety percent of the coral along twenty-four miles of Guam's 100-mile coastline in the past two and a half years. Australia's 1,250 mile-long Great Barrier Reef is now threatened, 300 miles of it now nearly dead.[2]

The menace of the "crown-of-thorns" is rapidly spreading throughout the Trust Territory. The U.S. is promoting a research project managed by the Westinghouse Ocean Research Laboratory of San Diego, California and a program to control this creeping disaster which threatens the very existence of islands, atolls and their valuable reefs. To date, control means are still inadequate, being limited to the killing of individual starfish by divers, usually armed with formaldehyde-injecting spears. The problem grows more acute constantly and has prompted an urgent combined research program between Australia and the United States.

An interesting article written by Richard H. Chesher in *Oceans*, No. 5, 1970, provides a vivid description of the Acanthaster and the problem it has created. Two U.S. Congressmen have proposed an all-out war on this predator to save the valuable coral reefs of the Pacific. Time is of the essence, they say.

The Marshallese are somewhat like the Polynesians in physical characteristics, with brown skin darker than that of the Samoans. Generally, they have straight black hair whereas the Polynesians' hair is wavy or curly.[3]

The total Marshallese population is 18,925, having increased by 7,000 since 1954. Modern health measures, fewer losses of lives at sea, and abolishment of abortion and infanticide all contribute to the rising population which now increases at a rate over three percent annually. The problem of over-population in the near future is a distinct probability. The table on the following page presents the Marshallese population by island or political subdivision.

The ancient pattern of life in the Marshalls has been significantly changed by the one and a half centuries of exposure to European and American trade, a century of missionary effort, and foreign rule under Spanish, German, Japanese and American administrators. Their once hardy self-reliance has, in part, succumbed to dependence on outside resources and even more for direction and authority. Many of the Marshall Islands have notable numbers of people of mixed nationalities.

Island or Political subdivision	Male	Female	Total
Ailinglapalap	611	584	1,195
Ailuk	200	184	384
Arno	664	609	1,273
Aur	184	179	361
Ebon	434	401	835
Jaluit	573	554	1,113
Kili	146	163	309
Kwajalein (Ebeye)	1,780	1,760	3,540
Lae	63	68	131
Lib	80	62	142
Likiep	240	190	430
Majuro	2,631	2,619	5,250
Maloelap	246	248	494
Mjit	154	166	320
Mili	298	284	582
Namorik	291	256	547
Namu	326	271	597
Rongelap	100	89	189
Ujae	99	92	191
Ujelong	127	125	252
Utirik	133	135	268
Wotho	19	19	38
Wotje	214	182	396
Other Islands	47	41	88
Total	9,658	9,267	18,925

U.S. Dept. of State, *Trust Territory of the Pacific Islands Report by the United States to the United Nations* (Washington: U.S. Govt. Print. Off., 1967) p. 12.

Prior to World War II thatched houses predominated, but lumber and corrogated tin huts are now seen throughout the islands. The shanty-town slums which exist on Ebeye and Majuro Islands, of the Kwajalein and Majuro atolls respectively, are a shameful contrast to the handsomely land-scaped American oasis on Kwajalein Island itself, which will be discussed in greater detail later on.

In reflecting on the nature of early missionaries, a present-day missionary in the Marshalls recently said that "when they stopped burning witches in Salem, they [the witch hunters] came here."[4] Missionaries have carried on a crusade in the Marshalls since 1852 which has done all possible to change native life. They almost outlawed singing, dancing, and general ebulliance, but for all their efforts they have not succeeded in changing the Micronesian's devotion to and freedom of an active sex life. Today's missionaries are quite different than they were during the early Christian crusade in the Marshalls, and are genuinely respected and liked. Modern-day missionaries have contributed substantially to the social, economic, and educational advancement of the region.

The social order in the Marshalls has changed in recent times, but of course, the old social structure based on hereditary distinctions is still recognized, which establishes class membership by birth on the mother's side. A "iroij", or a paramount chief, is a iroij if his mother was iroij, regardless of the rank of his father. This custom stems from the relative unimportance of identifying the father. The U.S. at one time made it mandatory to register all births and parents, and many women were so uncertain of their children's fathers that they would report anyone's name—the district clerks in many areas are shown as the fathers of large portions of the youthful population.

There are still two main divisions in village society—nobility and commoners—but the old caste system is breaking down. In the past it was required that a paramount chief marry within his own caste, but this custom is less rigidly adhered to now. The atoll in the Marshalls has been the traditional standard of the well-defined social unit. This too is changing because of improved transportation between atolls and the fact that the people constantly shift residence. Consequently the atoll clan means much less today.[5]

The Micronesians possessed extraordinary maritime skill early in their history based on their ability to interpret the signs in the sea and the sky accurately. They developed an intricate cartography based upon scrutiny of the sea long before the Europeans developed celestial navigation. The crude, but accurate, charts were simple lattices of wood or coconut leaf midrib curved to show the swells and joined to show the swirls of the ocean currents. Cowrie shells marked the islands and leaf strips show the currents and navigational directions.

Because of their navigational skills the Marshallese were the farthest-ranging of all Oceanic peoples, variously reported as sailing from 600 to 1000 nautical miles away from home on their expeditions. They sent raiding parties to Kusaie, Truk, and were reported to have appeared in the Gilberts and even the Ellice island groups.[6]

In the Marshalls, land ownership and tenure, political and social life are interrelated and inseparable. The traditional form of government was headed by clan "iroij" (paramount chiefs) or "kings." Nobility related to the kings and queens were known as "iroij-irik" or "dukes" and "duchesses." The commoners consisted of a group of overseers known as "alab," and the workers were called "drijerbal" or "kajur," meaning subjects of the king.

This commoner class could not wear the distinctive tattoos of the nobility.[7]

The alab was a commoner supervisor for the king's lands parceled out by tenure to iroij-irik's (commoner's). The king always got "first fruit," the best of everything as his payment. In the late nineteenth century a system of shares was evolved which gave land tenure to every Marshallese upon birth. Thus land became, because it was so scarce, the single most important consideration in Marshallese society. When the Japanese controlled the islands, they initiated a policy which restricted chiefs from moving anyone off his own land at will, a practice which the U.S. has continued. Consequently, land tenure in essence now means ownership. However reefs which used to belong to chiefs have been declared to be in the public domain; otherwise the system of land ownership and tenure is unchanged.[8]

The Marshallese system of land ownership and tenure, identity, inheritance, and transfer (sale) is unusually complex. All four stratas of society (iroij, iroij-irik, alab, and kajur) become involved, sharing in a single "wato" (lot). Each wato is from one to five acres in size and usually runs across an island from lagoon side to ocean side.

Most of the High Commissioner's problems in the Marshalls have evolved from land issues. One such incident occurred in 1946 when the U.S., in preparation for nuclear tests, began to uproot the 312 persons then living in the Bikini and Eniwetok atolls. The Bikinians were relocated on the nearby uninhabited island of Rongerik and for the inconvenience were compensated with a $25,000 cash payment and a $300,000 trust fund. The island of Rongerik, however, according to native legend, had been cursed by the witch Libokra, who had contaminated all the food on the island and in the sea around it. The Bikinians nearly starved to death on Rongerik before the TTPI administrators realized their plight and again relocated them on the reefless, relatively tiny, remote, and austere island of Kili. The Bikinians are now mostly second generation since relocation, but have never been happy away from their homeland and want to return to it. The U.S. Government has promised to return them to Bikini when ecological conditions permit. No date has been determined for their return.

The Eniwetokese, who were less in number and had less land, were relocated to the island of Ujelang where they still live in relative contentment. They too were compensated with a cash settlement of $25,000, but, because less people and land were involved, received only a $150,000 trust fund. However, their population has grown from 146 persons to over 300.

Another such incident involved the land in the Kwajalein Atoll which the U.S. wanted for a missile site. The islanders were not compensated for many years because of an impasse in the settlement discussions. The U.S. initially offered to pay the islanders $250 per acre for indefinite use of the land. However, the native chief, a shrewd, young man named Amata Kabua, would not agree to what he considered to be a low price. Also he wanted a definite date specified for the return of the land to its owners. The U.S. would not agree to this stipulation, but Amata Kabua, with the help of lawyers, succeeded in getting a higher price for the land. On February 5, 1964 he accepted a check for $712,500.

The administrative center for the Marshall Islands District is on Majuro Island, in the Majuro Atoll which is in the Ratak chain of islands.

The only Micronesian to rise to a high office in the U.S. Administration of the TTPI is Dwight Heine, the son of a German missionary and his Marshallese wife. Heine is a graduate from the University of Hawaii and one of the first two Marshallese to attend an American university. Both of his parents were beheaded by the Japanese for refusing to swear alligence to the Emperor of Japan. Heine was elected to be the first speaker of the Micronesian General Assembly of the Congress of Micronesia. He is now the District Administrator of the Marshall Islands District.[9]

Micronesians are taken into Civil Service on a first opportunity basis through the San Francisco, Honolulu, or Guam registers, and although the qualifications are the same as for U.S. citizens, the job title and pay scale is keyed to some local index which sets Micronesians below Americans. This type of discrimination is deeply resented and is the *source of unrest* among ambitious young Micronesian leaders.

Traditional patterns of rule and order by hereditary chiefs has discouraged democratic political activity in the Marshalls, although spirited political campaigns have been held in the Marianas and Palaus. Recently, with the emergence of men like Dwight Heine, there is an awakening of democratic processes and political consciousness in the Marshalls. Four political parties exist in Micronesia and are represented in the Marshall Islands—the Liberal, Progressive, Popular, and Territorial Parties, the latter two being the most powerful.

Almost every island group in Micronesia has a different system of local hereditary rule. Consequently any elected government must either incorporate the hereditary ruling elite or show subservience to them in order to evade friction with the hereditary chiefs, many who hold considerable distinction and influence. Such a problem in the Marshalls, for example, involved a highly respected chief whom local politicians had convinced to run for election in the city council. The objective was to solve the problem of the council's fear of taking action because of their respect for his authority. The chief was elected to the council, but whenever anything controversial came up the chief refused to vote because, as he put it, "they were his children" and he didn't want to take sides. Consequently, nobody else would vote because they did not want to disagree with the old chief.[10]

Some self-confident, young Micronesians think they are ready for self-government now. Most of those who carry the local responsibilities, however, seem to think it will be a long time before they are ready.[11]

11 / The Pacific Islands: Summary and Conclusions

W. O. Miller,

Captain, Judge Advocate General's Corps, United States Navy

R. W. Thompson,

Captain, Supply Corps, United States Navy

The political history of the Pacific Islands has been turbulent, to say the least. During the late 19th and early 20th centuries, large island groups gradually became subject to the colonial administrations of one or another of the western powers. As the result of the peace conference following World War I, the colonial power balance in the Pacific was altered. Japan received the League of Nations mandate for all the former German islands north of the equator—the Marianas, Carolines and Marshall Islands. Australia received the mandate for the islands south of the equator, with the exception of Western Samoa which went to New Zealand. Under the mandates system, fortification was not permitted and annual reports were required. In the Washington Conference of 1921–1922 the Anglo-Japanese Alliance was replaced by a Four-Power Agreement of the United States, Britain, France and Japan, which affirmed mutual respect for each other's possessions and a continuation of the status quo.

In the Five-Power Treaty Agreement, in addition to naval limitations, the decision was reached that the status quo in regard to fortification and naval bases would be maintained. Formalized naval tonnages of capital ships became less meaningful with the increased capabilities of submarines and aircraft. The technical benefits provided by the conference were circumvented by the changing status of technology.

The immediate result of the treaties was that Japan's security and influence in the western Pacific was enhanced three ways: she could keep her naval bases which were stronger than those on the other islands, she was protected from other powers by the non-fortification agreement, and she received the mandates. All of these were strategically beneficial near her home waters. Britain profited by the right to fortify Singapore, Australia, and New Zealand beyond the restricted zone. The U.S., by its agreement, failed to gain any strength in the western Pacific to back up its Far East policies, while at home domestic politics prevented the Navy from maintaining the numbers and types of ships authorized. The conferences contributed to stabilization of the Pacific area during the 1920's, but did not stop later expansion and the resultant instability in the area. The views of U.S. naval strategic planners at the end of World War I, that the Micronesian Islands lay across vital lines of communications to the Far East and should not be allowed to fall under Japanese control were borne out by the subsequent loss of control in the entire western Pacific during World War II.

In accordance with the World War II peace settlement, Japan was removed from all territories outside of her main four islands. A Trust Territory of the Pacific Islands, including the Marshalls, Carolines and Marianas, was placed under the United States as a "strategic trusteeship," serving both security and humanitarian principles. Under this designation the United States was given complete control, including the rights of exclusion, control over air traffic, and the most-favored-nation economic privilege under the auspices of the Security Council of the United Nations. Other trusteeships accountable to the General Assembly were also created in the South Pacific with Australia as the administering power of the Trust Territory of New Guinea and Nauru and New Zealand the administering power of Western Samoa. There also were many island groupings which remained under the control of western colonial powers and which were not incorporated into the trusteeship system. The provisions of the United Nations Charter, however, made it clear that all of these dependent areas—both those coming under Trusteeship Council supervision and those remaining under the direct unilateral control of the former colonial power—were now considered wards of the international community as a whole, and that the principle of self-determination of peoples was applicable to them all.

It is this latter provision of the Charter—Article 73—which forms the basis for the current discussions and debates about the fidelity of the administering powers to their trusts and over the political future of the remaining dependent territories. While it is true that only two trust territories remain in the Pacific—the Pacific Islands and New Guinea—there are still at least twelve other dependent territories under the administration of colonial powers. They are Timor, Brunei, Fiji, Niue, Tokelau, Papua, American Samoa, Guam, New Hebrides, Gilbert and Ellice Islands, Solomon Islands and Pitcairn Island. This does not consider French Polynesia which is regarded by France as an Overseas Department rather than a dependent territory—an opinion not concurred in by the U.N.

In late 1960, responding to the prodding of the Soviet Union, the General Assembly adopted Resolution 1514 (XV), which condemned the continued existence of colonial regimes and asserted that immediate steps should be taken by the colonial powers to transfer all powers of administration to the peoples of the dependent territories. The following year, noting that little progress had been made in the implementation of this resolution, the General Assembly, again responding to the prodding of the Soviet Union, created a Special Committee to inquire into this matter and to make suggestions and recommendations concerning it. This Special Committee, now known as the "Committee of Twenty-Four" has become the principal mechanism through which the United Nations seeks to oversee the implementation of the principle of self-determination in dependent territories.

In 1964 the United Nations' Committee of Twenty-Four began to give serious attention first to the question of the Pacific Island dependencies. The anti-colonialist bias of the committee—a full two-thirds of the Committee are either Communist or representatives of former colonial states— has been consistently reflected in both the Committee's methods of work and in the reports which it has submitted to the General Assembly. Committee recommendations since 1964 have resulted in a series of General Assembly resolutions which, in even more deprecatory language, condemn the administration of the administering powers, assert that colonialism is incompatible with the Charter of the U.N., reiterate that the maintenance of military bases in dependent areas is incompatible with the principles and the purposes of the Charter, and insist that the administering powers take immediate steps to provide for the "complete independence" of the peoples of all these dependent territories.

Whether or not such stringent requirements are approved of by the majority of the Twenty-Four, it is quite apparent that the Committee has allowed itself to be used as a forum for propaganda assaults on the Western powers. This is particularly evident in the Committee's treatment of the Pacific Islands, treatment which seems to have degenerated into a vendetta against western military bases in the Pacific Island territories particularly those belonging to the U.S. As a result of Soviet leadership, and the enthusiastic following of the former colonial members, the Committee of Twenty-Four has, since 1965, roundly condemned the presence of military bases in the Pacific territories as existing for aggressive and repressive purposes. The Committee resolved that the bases should be dismantled and all military activity in these areas should cease. Their efforts have been affirmatively endorsed by the General Assembly in several resolutions which have repeated the same criticisms and recommendations.

This insistence by the General Assembly that military activity in the dependent territories should cease, and that steps should be taken forthwith to provide for the "complete independence" of the Pacific territories, poses a critical problem not only for the western administering powers but also for the dependent peoples themselves. Many of the leaders in these areas recognize the sociological difficulties involved. The cultural gap between the western powers, for example, and New Guinea, makes it difficult to believe that there can be any rapid progress toward viable independence, and it is by no means clear whether in any case the various indigenous societies of the Pacific would opt for independence.

There are further problems because of traditional social structures and the diverse ethnic differences within island groups. This is true even on some individual islands. Resurging population growth, and a relatively static economy and infra-structure are adding to social problems. The progress in secondary education in some areas, notably the United States trust territory, has been criticized on the basis that economic and political realities are not living up to aspirations. Vocational training and economic investment to encourage local work, enterprise, and development are the most urgent needs. Tourist trade, sea resources, and selected agricultural products such as copra offer greatest potential for economic growth. A transportation infra-structure is required to link the scattered islands for cohesive economic effort and political progress. At best, however, these efforts promise internal viability to only some island areas, and even this lies far in the future.

In addition to the afore-mentioned differences among many groups, the history of those populations in close proximity is marked with conflicts and instability. The political future of present island groupings can be considered in regard to internal and external factors. Internally, some islands will be capable of eventual self-government much sooner than others. In Micronesia the United States has been building slowly from the "ground up" toward this end. However, the islands still need outside guidance at the territorial level in external matters relating to defense, economy, and foreign relations. Despite obstacles in the U.N. and the islands themselves, a logical development for Micronesia would be a single federation of the different island groups with Guam as the seat of government. The trend in the Marianas is toward this type of merger. The United States can assist in political and economic development by continuing association through AID-type programs and providing for security.

The same situation exists in other areas where there is some common interests among the peoples, even if this identity is only an outgrowth of their association with a single administering power. Because of their lack of independent viability, some sort of association with a stronger power will be required for many years to come. Maturing political opinion in these areas will- come to recognize this, and self-determination in these areas should result in decisions to follow the lead of the Cook Islanders, who in 1965 opted for local internal autonomy but with a continuance of political ties with the former administering power.

As the self-determination process matures, and as various island groupings select their own options for a political future, there seems to be little doubt that Japan will begin to play a much more significant role in their economic future. Japan has been moving cautiously toward a wider leadership role in Asia. She is expected soon to rank as the world's third strongest economic power, trailing only the U.S. and the U.S.S.R. She will undoubtably want to play a greater role economically, diplomatically, and militarily in the future in Asia. As the prime minister of one neighboring country expressed it: "The Japanese are a great people, and no great people will accept as their destiny making better transistor radios and teaching the underdeveloped how to grow better rice." Recent U.S. overtures toward China, undertaken without consultation with Japanese authorities, and U.S. economic initiatives which the Japanese regard as unduly restrictive, may well hasten the pace of Japan's advance toward determination of her own place in Asia—and in the world.

It is estimated that the day will come, probably within the next five to ten years, when Japan will assume the responsibility for providing for her own security. By that time, or even before, it is possible that the United States will lose its existing base rights in Japan and Okinawa. This situation will significantly increase the strategic importance of the Territory of the Pacific Islands to the U.S. and to Japan. The situation would become quite similar to that existing prior to World War II with these islands playing an important strategic role.

The continued control or predominant use of these islands by the U.S. could still cause tension between the two countries. Without bases in Japan the U.S. would probably find it necessary to rely on some of these islands as secondary or tertiary defensive positions. Japan may not welcome the establishment of such bases, particularly strategic bases, so close to her home islands. Accordingly, the U.S. will have to work toward continued friendship and cooperation with Japan to ensure that any extended military use made of the islands does not bring the two countries toward another confrontation. The cooperation could certainly include assistance from Japan in building a viable economic base, where feasible, in the islands, and strong efforts to keep the other Asian interests of Japan and the U.S. on a parallel course.

With the advent of the U.N. trusteeships, Japanese participation in the economic life of the Pacific Islands was virtually eliminated and has only recently begun to emerge as an important factor. Some Japanese fishing has continued in the area and more recently there have been some controlled Japanese projects in the Pacific trust territory. These include phosphate mining operation in the Carolines and a small freighter service between Japan, Guam, and the island district centers. Projects of this type were prohibited prior to 1962. In 1967 air service was started between Guam and Tokyo.

In 1966 Japan played a key role in the establishment of the thirty-two member Asian Development Bank set up in Manila, with a planned initial capitalization of one billion dollars. Tokyo matched the U.S. contribution of two hundred million dollars and a Japanese banker became the first president. Japan also proposed and hosted the first Southest Asia Economic Development Conference, a nine-nation meeting in Tokyo that sought ways for economic cooperation.

With this continuing and growing economic activity, its prewar history of economic development of the island groups, Japanese participation in the economy of the islands will undoubtedly be a factor in the future. The degree of this participation, however, will probably depend upon the determination in each area of its political future.

In summary, it must be said that strategic considerations continue to be the determinative factor in the future of the Pacific Islands. Cries of "imperialism" and "neo-colonialism" are likely to be heard from the Soviet Union, whose long-term interests envisage the denial to the western powers of a Pacific military presence. This rhetoric will probably also continue to find support from the "third world" members of the U.N. until such time as the western powers are able to demonstrate that the best interests of the islanders, themselves, is association with the administering power and not "complete independence." Hence, the critical problem for the western powers in this area is to take such actions in their respective territories as necessary to convince the islanders that they have an identity of interests with their administering power. The international pressures for self-determination can be resisted for a time, but ultimately the colonial powers must implement this concept which, after all, is a product of western philosophy and statesmanship. Only through this type of identity of interest and free association with the western powers can the political future of the Pacific Islands be determined consistent with western strategic interests.

Sources

1 / The United Nations and Oceania

1. Douglas L. Oliver, *The Pacific Islands* (Cambridge: Harvard University Press, 1958).
2. Samuel E. Morison, *Strategy and Compromise* (Boston: Little, Brown, 1958), p. 86.
3. Harold H. Sprout and Margaret T. Sprout, *Toward a New Order of Sea Power* (Princeton: Princeton University Press, 1940), Chap. I.
4. For example, see discussions in Leland M. Goodrich, *The United Nations* (New York: Crowell, 1959), p. 294–96; and Inis L. Claude, Jr., *Swords into Plowshares* (New York: Random House, 1956), p. 346–48.
5. Goodrich, p. 297.
6. G. S. Windass, "Power Politics and Ideals; the Principle of Self Determination," *International Relations*, October 1966, p. 177.
7. Charter of the United Nations, Art. 76.
8. Charter of the United Nations, Art. 73.
9. *Ibid.*, Art. 86.
10. *Ibid.*, Art. 77.
11. United Nations, General Assembly, *The United Nations and Decolonization* (New York: 1965), p. 2.
12. Charter, Arts. 86, 87.
13. Claude, p. 356.
14. United Nations, *Yearbook of the United Nations 1960* (New York: Columbia University Press, 1960), p. 47.
15. *The United Nations and Decolonization*, p. 9.
16. David A. Kay, ed., "The Politics of Decolonization: the New Nations and the United Nations Political Process," *International Organization*, Fall 1967, p. 786.
17. United Nations, General Assembly, *Official Records: Plenary Meetings*, A/4502, 15th session (New York: 23 September 1960), v. I, p. I, p. 74.
18. United Nations, General Assembly, *Official Records*, A/4502, 15th session, agenda item 87, corr. 1 (New York: 23 September 1960), annex v. II.
19. *United Nations Yearbook 1960*, p. 45.

20. *Ibid.*, p. 48.

21. Harold K. Jacobson, "The U.N. and Colonialism," David A. Kay, ed., *The United Nations Political System* (New York: Wiley, 1967), p. 314.

22. United Nations, General Assembly, Special Committee . . . on the Granting of Independence to Colonial Countries and Peoples, *Summary Record*, A/AC.109/SR576 (New York: 13 March 1968), p. 17.

23. Rupert Emerson, "Colonialism, Political Development and the U.N.," Norman J. Padelford and Leland M. Goodrich, eds., *The United Nations in the Balance* (New York: Praeger, 1965), p. 129.

24. *United Nations Yearbook 1960*, p. 48–50.

25. Rupert Emerson, *Self Determination Revisited in the Era of Decolonization* (Cambridge: Harvard University, Center for International Affairs, 1964), p. 3.

27. *Ibid.*, p. 56.

26. *United Nations Yearbook 1961*, p. 45.

28. *United Nations Yearbook 1963*, p. 441.

29. *United Nations Yearbook 1960*, p. 51.

30. *United Nations Yearbook 1962*, p. 60.

31. United Nations Yearbook 1964, p. 422–434.

32. *Ibid.*, p. 403–410.

33. *Ibid.*, p. 409.

34. *Ibid.*, p. 430.

35. *United Nations Yearbook 1960*, p. 509.

36. *United Nations Yearbook 1965*, p. 574.

37. "Trust Territory of Nauru," *U.N. Monthly Chronicle*, January 1968, p. 81.

38. *United Nations Yearbook 1965*, p. 588.

39. *Ibid.*, p. 554.

40. *Ibid.*, p. 538, 542, 546.

41. *United Nations Yearbook 1966*, p. 558, 594; "Text of Resolution A/RES/2326 (XXII)," *U.N. Monthly Chronicle*, January 1968, p. 77; "Territories Not Considered Separately," *U. N. Monthly Chronicle*, January 1968, p. 83.

42. "Special Committee of Twenty-four," *U. N. Monthly Chronicle*, March 1967, p. 20–23.

43. United Nations, General Assembly, Special Committee, *Summary Record*, A/AC.109/SR. 564 (New York: 2 January 1968). p. 10.

44. United Nations, General Assembly, Special Committee, Subcommittee I, *Summary Record*, A/AC.109/SC.2/SR44 (New York: 24 November 1967), p. 9–10.

45. United Nations, General Assembly, Special Committee, *Summary Record*, A/AC.109/SR.574 (New York: 3 April 1968), p. 5–7.

46. United Nations, General Assembly, Special Committee, *Summary Record*, A/AC.109/SR.576 (New York: 13 March 1968), p. 2–7. [NOTE: Since this chapter was written both the United States and the United Kingdom have withdrawn from participation in the Committee of Twenty-four, U.N. doc. A/8277, *The Deparment of State Bulletin*, 8 February 1971, p. 186; U.N. Monthly Chronicle, Vol. VIII, No. 3, March, 1971, p. 7.]

47. *Summary Record*, A/AC.109/SR.574, p. 5–7.

48. United Nations, General Assembly, Special Committee, *Summary Record*, A/AC.109/SR.577 (New York: 15 March 1968), p. 9.

49. United Nations, General Assembly, Special Committee, Subcommittee I, *Summary Record*, A/AC.109/SC.2/SR55 (New York: 27 August 1968), p. 59.

50. *Ibid.*, p. 56.

51. United Nations, General Assembly, Special Committee, Subcommittee I, *Summary Record*, A/AC.109/SR.47–56 (New York: 27 August 1968), p. 48.

52. *Ibid.*

2 / Trust Territories of Melanesia

1. "Age of Trust," *International Affairs*, Vol. *XXII* (London: Royal Institute of International Affairs, 1946), p. 201.

2. W. P. Morrell, *Britain in the Pacific Islands* (Oxford: Clarendon Press, 1960), p. 431.

3. Harold H. and Margaret T. Sprout, *Toward a New Order of Sea Power* (Princeton, N.J.: Princeton University Press, 1940), p. 33.

4. Guy H. Scholefield, *The Pacific, Its Past and Future* (London: Murray, 1919), p. 305.

5. C. Hartley Grattan, *The Southwest Pacific Since 1900* (Ann Arbor, Mich.: University of Michigan Press, 1963), p. 417.

6. C. Brunsdon Fletcher, *The Problem of the Pacific* (New York: Holt, 1919), p. 86.

7. *Ibid.*, p. 48.

8. Gratten, p. 55.

9. Fletcher, p. xxi–xxvix.

10. David Lloyd George, *Memoirs of the Peace Conference* (New Haven: Yale, 1939), p. 32.

11. "Wilson Defends Treaty," *Christian Science Monitor* (Boston), 11 July 1919, p. 22:1.

12. Freda White, *Mandates* (London: Jonathan Cape, 1926), p. 14.

13. Lloyd George, p. 345–346.

14. "Guide to League of Nations Publications" (New York: Columbia, 1951), p. 152–153.

15. Lloyd George, p. 364–365.

16. *Ibid.*, p. 360.

17. Gratten, p. 72.

18. *Ibid.*, p. 419.

19. *Ibid.*, p. 520.

20. Norman Bentwich, *The Mandate System* (London: Longmans, Green, 1930), p. 101.

21. Gratten, p. 454.

22. *Ibid.*

23. J. G. Starke, *The ANZUS Treaty Alliance* (Carlton: Melbourne University Press, 1965), p. 8.

24. *Ibid.*, p. 10.

25. Alan S. Watt, *The Evolution of Australian Foreign Policy 1938–1965* (London: Cambridge University Press, 1967), p. 76.

26. Starke, p. 16.

27. Trevor R. Reese, *Australia in the Twentieth Century* (New York: Praeger, 1964), p. 130.

28. George Thullen, *Problems of the Trusteeship System* (Geneva: Librairie Droz, 1964), p. 41.

29. Starke, p. 18.

30. Bernard K. Gordon, *New Zealand Becomes a Pacific Power* (Chicago: University of Chicago Press, 1960), p. 215.

31. Watt, p. 91.

32. Günther Doeker, *The Treaty-Making Powers in the Commonwealth of Australia* (The Hague: Martinus Nijhoff, 1966), p. 153.

33. "Japanese Attack New Guinea," *The Times Weekly Edition* (London), 11 February 1942, p. 2:1.

34. Gratten, p. 547.

35. "United Nations Trusteeship Council," *Official Records* (New York), 29 June 1948, p. 134.

36. Gratten, p. 549.
37. "United Nations Review" (New York), June 1960, p. 48.
38. *Ibid.*, p. 50.
39. "Nauru Granted Independence," *The New York Times* (New York), 1 February 1968, p. 3:2.
40. *Ibid.*, 9 February 1968, p. 26:3.
41. *Ibid.*, 3 January 1962, p. 2:3; Gratten, p. 557.
42. "Western Samoa," *The New York Times* (New York), 18 September 1966, p. 12:1.

3 / The Samoan Islands

1. See especially Douglas L. Oliver, *The Pacific Islands* (Garden City: Doubleday, 1951), p. 331.
2. Guy H. Scholefield, *The Pacific, Its Past and Future* (London: John Murray, 1919), p. 148.
3. Felix M. Keesing, *Modern Samoa* (London: George Allen and Unwin, Ltd., 1934), p. 11.
4. "The Samoan Islands," *Encyclopaedia Americana*, International Edition (New York: American Corp., 1966), p. 223–227.
5. Keesing, p. 20.
6. *Ibid.*, p. 15.
7. Herman R. Friis, ed., *Pacific Basin; A History of Its Exploration*, American Geographical Society Special Publication No. 38 (New York: American Geographical Society, 1967), p. 166.
8. Alexander George Findlay, *South Pacific Ocean Directory* (London: Richard Holmes Laurie, 1863), p. 487.
9. Clyde H. Metcalf, *A History of the U.S. Marine Corps* (New York: G. P. Putnam, 1939), p. 93.
10. C. Hartley Grattan, *The Southwest Pacific to 1900* (Ann Arbor: University of Michigan Press, 1963), p. 483.
11. Scholefield, p. 149.
12. Lewis A. Kimberley, "Samoa and the Hurricane of March 1889," Papers of the Military Historical Society of Massachusetts, v. XII: *Naval Actions and History* (Boston: Griffith-Stillings Press, 1902).
13. Scholefield, p. 169.
14. Dudley W. Knox, *History of the U.S. Navy* (New York: Putnam and Son, 1936), p. 326; quoted from *New York Herald*, 9 March 1889.
15. W. E. Livezey, *Mahan on Sea Power* (Norman: University of Oklahoma Press, 1947), p. 202, 218.
16. Navy Department, *Annual Report*, 1889 (Washington: U.S. Govt. Print. Off.).
17. Herrick, p. 57–58.
18. Scholefield, p. 171.
19. *Ibid.*, p. 177.
20. Scholefield, p. 178.
21. Robert W. Robson, *The Pacific Islands Handbook 1944* (New York: Macmillan, 1945), p. 51.
22. Robson, p. 52.
23. *Ibid.*, p. 53.
24. T. C. Larkin, ed., *New Zealand External Relations*, Wellington, New Zealand, Institute of Public Administration Study No. 8 (London: Oxford University Press, 1962), p. 138.

25. James W. Davidson, "The Transition to Independence; The Example of Western Samoa," *The Australian Journal of Politics and History,* v. VII, no. 1 (May 1961), p. 23.

26. "Western Samoa Restricting Ties," *The New York Times,* 30 August 1964, p. 9:1.

27. Tillman Durden, "Western Samoa Slowly Accepting Outside," *The New York Times,* 28 August 1966, p. 17:3.

28. Frank Railinson, "Growth Plan Set for West Samoa," *The New York Times,* 7 February 1965, p. 10:1.

29. "Western Samoa Faces Problems," *The New York Times,* 14 January 1962, p. 31:1.

30. Tillman Durden, "Samoans Say U.S. Won't Give Help," *The New York Times,* 18 September 1966, p. 12:1.

31. U.S. Committee on Interior and Insular Affairs, 87th Congress, 1st Session, Report no. 38 (Washington: U.S. Govt. Print. Off., 1961), p. 21.

32. Clarence W. Hall, "Samoa: America's Shame in the South Seas," *Reader's Digest,* July 1961, p. 113.

33. J. A. C. Gray, *Amerika Samoa* (Annapolis: U.S. Naval Institute, 1960), p. 257, 258.

34. F. J. West, *Political Advancement in the South Pacific* (Melbourne: Oxford University Press, 1961), p. 136.

35. Clarence W. Hall, "Samoa: America's Showplace of the South Seas," *Reader's Digest,* November 1965, v. 87, no. 523, p. 157.

36. "American Samoa Called Neglected," *The New York Times,* 1 July 1961, p. 3:6.

37. "Problems of U.S. Territories Reviewed by Government Panels," *The New York Times,* 9 November 1961, p. 13:1.

38. Hall, "Samoa, America's Showplace . . . ," p. 159.

39. *Ibid.,* p. 166.

40. Tillman Durdin, "Prospering American Samoa is Emerging as a Showcase of the South Seas," *The New York Times,* 24 August 1966, p. 5:1.

41. Tillman Durdin, "Union of 2 Samoans Appears Unlikely," *The New York Times,* 9 October 1966, p. 38:1.

42. "U.N. Group Says U.S. Lags in Samoan Rule," *The New York Times,* 19 September 1964, p. 4:4.

43. Hall, "Samoa, America's Showplace . . . ," p. 168.

4 / New Guinea

1. For an excellent summary of the circumstances which attended the proclamation of the Protectorate, see Guy H. Scholefield, *The Pacific: Its Past and Future* (London: John Murray, 1917), p. 132–133.

2. Robert P. Thompson, *A National History of Australia, New Zealand and the Adjacent Islands* (London: George Routledge and Sons, 1919), p. 310.

3. Quoted in Paul W. van der Veur, "New Guinea Annexations and the Origin of the Irian Boundary," *Australian Outlook,* December 1964, p. 324.

4. Brian Essai, *Papua and New Guinea* (Melbourne: Oxford University Press, 1961), p. 10.

5. W. J. Hudson, "Australia's Experience as a Mandatory Power," *Australian Outlook,* April 1965, p. 35.

6. Scholefield, Guy H., *The Pacific: Its Past and Future* (London: Murray, 1919), p. 304.

7. U.S. Dept. of State, *Papers Relating to the Foreign Relations of the United States, 1918, Supp. I, The World War* (Washington: U.S. Govt. Print. Off., 1933), v. I, p. 16.

8. For an authoritative analysis of the origins of the mandates idea, see Wm. Roger Louis, "The South West African Origins of the Sacred Trust," *African Affairs*, January 1967; *Great Britain and Germany's Lost Colonies 1914–1919* (London: Oxford University Press, 1967).

9. Rupert Emerson, *From Empire to Nation* (Boston: Beacon Press, 1960), p. 24.

10. Hudson, p. 36.

11. United Nations, Department of Public Information, *Yearbook of the United Nations 1946–1947* (Lake Success, New York: United Nations, 1947), p. 576.

12. Dwight D. Eisenhower, *Waging Peace* (Garden City, New York: Doubleday, 1965), p. 572.

13. Quoted in D. C. Corbett, "Problems of Australian Foreign Policy," *The Australian Journal of Politics and History*, May 1961, p. 11.

14. United Nations, Department of Public Information, *The United Nations in West New Guinea* (New York: United Nations, 1963), p. 4.

15. *Ibid.*, p. 4, 29.

16. Quoted in J. D. Legge, "Problems of Australian Foreign Policy," *The Australian Journal of Politics and History*, November 1960, p. 150.

17. F. J. West, "The New Guinea Question: An Australian View," *Foreign Affairs*, April 1961, p. 504.

18. See for example Legge, p. 150; "Australia: Geographical Basis of Foreign Policy," *The Round Table*, March 1965, p. 177; "Australia: Our Mandate in New Guinea," *The Round Table*, September 1964, p. 402; and J. A. C. MacKee, "Inflation and Confrontation in Indonesia," *Australian Outlook*, December 1964, p. 278.

19. Margaret Mead, "The Rights of Primitive Peoples," *Foreign Affairs*, January 1967, p. 306.

20. For an appraisal of general conditions in Papua-New Guinea, see J. R. Kerr, "Higher Education in New Guinea," *Australian Outlook*, December 1964, p. 266; and R. T. Shand, "Some Obstacles to the Economic Development of Papua-New Guinea," *Australian Outlook*, December 1963, p. 306.

21. For a thorough discussion of the political future of the territory as viewed from two different points in the recent past, see J. R. Kerr, "The Political Future of New Guinea," *Australian Outlook*, September 1959, p. 181; and Paul W. van der Veur, "The Political Future of Papua-New Guinea," *Australian Outlook*, August 1966, p. 200.

5 / Micronesia and Self-Determination

1. Emil J. Sady, *The United Nations and Dependent Peoples* (Washington: Brookings Institution, 1956), p. 3–14.

2. U.S. Department of State, *Trust Territory of the Pacific Islands Under United States Administration*, Annual Report by the United States to the United Nations for the year 1960 (Washington: Govt. Print. Off., 1961), p. 41.

3. United Nations, General Assembly Resolution 1514 (XV) of 14 December 1960.

4. U.S. Dept. of State, *U.S. Participation in the UN*, Report by the President to the Congress for the year 1961 (Washington: U.S. Govt. Print. Off., 1962), p. 34.

5. *Ibid.*, p. 55.

6. United Nations, General Assembly, Official Records: Sixteenth Session, Supplement No. 17 (A/5100), *Resolutions adopted by the General Assembly during its Sixteenth Session*, Vol. 1. (New York: 1962), p. 65.

7. United Nations, General Assembly, Official Records: Seventeenth Session, Supplement No. 17 (A/5217), *Resolutions adopted by the General Assembly during its Seventeenth Session* (New York: 1962), p. 72–73.

8. Rupert Emerson, *Africa and United States Policy* (Englewood Cliffs: Prentice Hall, 1967), p. 32.

9. State, *U. S. Participation in the UN*, 1964, p. 234.

10. *The New York Times*, 6 January 1968, p. 11:1.

11. *The New York Times*, 28 January 1967, p. 7:3.

12. Rupert Emerson, *From Empire to Nation* (Boston: Beacon Press, 1962), p. 297.

13. Rupert Emerson, *Self-Determination Revisited in the Era of Decolonization*, (Cambridge: Center for International Affairs, Harvard University, 1966), p. 27.

14. *Ibid.*, p. 64.

15. Sady, p. 175.

16. State, *U.S. Participation in the UN*, 1961, p. 308.

17. State, *Trust Territory*, 1962, p. 17.

18. State, *U.S. Participation in the UN*, 1963, p. 312.

19. U.S. Congress, House, Committee on Interior and Insular Affairs, *Promoting the Economic and Social Development of the Trust Territory of the Pacific Islands*, Report (Washington: U.S. Govt. Print. Off., 1963), p. 6.

20. State, *U.S. Participation in the UN*, 1964, p. 223–227.

21. *Ibid.*, p. 235.

22. *Ibid.*, p. 224.

23. State, *U.S. Participation in the UN*, 1965, p. 267.

24. State, *U.S. Participation in the UN*, 1967, p. 186–187.

25. United Nations, General Assembly, Report of the Special Committee, *Trust Territory of the Pacific Islands*, A/7200/Add.9 (New York: 1968), p. 114.

26. *UN Monthly Chronicle*, June 1968, p. 108.

27. *UN Monthly Chronicle*, July 1968, p. 59.

28. United Nations, General Assembly, Special Committee, Provisional Summary Record of the One Hundred and Fourth Meeting, *Trust Territory of the Pacific Islands*, A/AC.109/L.585 (New York: 1968), p. 3.

29. William M. Blair, "Hickel Departs for Micronesia," *The New York Times*, 2 May 1969, p. 9:1.

30. Robert Trumbull, "Micronesians Get Self-Rule Pledge," *The New York Times*, 6 May 1969, p. 13:1.

31. Robert Trumbull, "Micronesians Ask Loose Ties to U.S.," *The New York Times*, 7 May 1969, p. 15:1.

32. Robert Trumbull, "Micronesian Aides, in Saipan, Plan Future," *The New York Times*, 11 May 1969, p. 2:3.

33. Kathleen Teltsch, "U.S. Tells U.N. of Plans for Developing Micronesia," *The New York Times*, 9 June 1969, p. 5:3.

34. Robert Trumbull, "Panel in Micronesia Suggests Eventual Merger With Guam," *The New York Times*, 25 July 1969, p. 6:4.

35. Robert Trumbull, "Guam's Voters Oppose Proposal to Merge With the Northern Marianas Islands," *The New York Times*, 5 November 1969, p. 19:3.

36. Robert Trumbull, "Marianas Voice Desire to Join Guam," *The New York Times*, 10 November 1969, p. 8:4.

37. United Nations, General Assembly, Special Committee, *Summary Record of the Forty-seventh to the Fifty-sixth Sessions*, A/AC.109/SC.2/SR. 47–56 (New York: 1968) p. 49.

38. *The New York Times*, 11 May 1969, p. 2:3.

39. UNGA A/7200, p. 15.

6 / American Involvement in Perspective

1. Walter Millis, ed., *The Forrestal Diaries* (New York: Viking, 1951), p. 214.
2. Cordell Hull, *The Memoirs of Cordell Hull*, v. II (New York: Macmillan, 1948), p. 1109–10.
3. *U.S. Dept. of State Bulletin*, v. 9, 4 December 1943, p. 393.
4. Millis, p. 8.
5. Hull, p. 1466.
6. U.S. Dept. of State, *Foreign Relations of the United States: The Conferences at Malta and Yalta, 1945* (Washington: U.S. Govt. Print. Off., 1955), p. 78–81.
7. *Ibid.*, p. 844.
8. Ruth B. Russell, *A History of the United Nations Charter* (Washington: Brookings Institution, 1958), p. 576–579.
9. Millis, p. 33.
10. Russell, p. 586–589.
11. Dorothy E. Richards, *United States Naval Administration of the Trust Territories of the Pacific Islands* (Washington: U.S. Govt. Print. Off., 1963, v. III, p. 3–5.
12. Millis, p. 130–131.
13. Secretary Ickes, as quoted by Richards, p. 18–19.
14. *Ibid.*, p. 19–20.
15. Millis, p. 232.
16. James F. Byrnes, *Speaking Frankly* (New York: Harper, 1947), p. 219.
17. United Nations, *Yearbook*, 1960 (New York: U.N. Office of Public Information, 1961), p. 45.
18. "U.N. Unit Supports U.S. on Micronesia," *The New York Times*, 13 July 1966, p. 19:6.

7 / Japan and the Mandates

1. Merlo J. Pusey, *Charles Evans Hughes* (New York: Columbia University Press, 1963), p. 451.
2. Paul H. Clyde, *Japan's Pacific Mandate* (New York: Macmillan, 1935), p. 37.
3. *Ibid.*, p. 38–39.
4. Huntington Gilchrist, "The Japanese Islands: Annexation or Trusteeships?," *Foreign Affairs*, July 1944, p. 637. See also C. Hartley Grattan, "Those Japanese Mandates," *Harpers Magazine*, January 1944.
5. Pusey, p. 449 and Dorothy Borg, *The United States and the Far Eastern Crisis of 1933–1938* (Cambridge, Mass.: Harvard University Press, 1964), p. 236.
6. Earl S. Pomeroy, "American Policy Respecting the Marshalls, Carolines, and Marianas 1898–1941," *Pacific Historical Review*, February 1948, p. 49.
7. *Ibid.*, p. 49.
8. *Ibid.*
9. Lieutenant Colonel P. N. Pierce, "The Unsolved Mystery of Pete Ellis," *Marine Corps Gazette*, February 1962, p. 36.
10. *Ibid.*, p. 35–40.
11. Captain Ellis M. Zacharias, U.S.N., *Secret Missions* (New York: Putnam Sons, 1946), p. 39–50.
12. Pomeroy, p. 49.
13. *Ibid.*, p. 50.
14. Richard N. Current, *Secretary Stimson, A Study in Statecraft* (New Brunswick: Rutgers University Press, 1954), p. 70.
15. Borg, p. 236.
16. *Ibid.*, p. 236–237.

17. *Ibid.*, p. 237.
18. Gilchrist, p. 640.
19. *Ibid.*
20. Borg, p. 237–238.
21. Gilchrist, p. 640.
22. Joseph C. Grew, *Ten Years in Japan* (New York: Simon and Schuster, 1944),
p. 85.
23. Borg, p. 239.
24. *Ibid.*, p. 240.
25. Gilchrist, p. 640.
26. Borg, p. 252.
27. Pusey, p. 451.
28. *Ibid.*, p. 452.
29. Clyde, p. 202–224.
30. Willard Price, *Japan's Islands of Mystery* (New York: Day, 1944), p. 183.
31. Gilchrist, p. 638.
32. Lieutenant General Masatake Okumiya, "For Sugar Boats or Submarines?,"
United States Naval Institute Proceedings, August 1968, p. 67.
33. *Ibid.*, p. 72–73.
34. *Ibid.*, p. 70.
35. *Ibid.*, p. 71.
36. *Ibid.*
37. *Ibid.*, p. 69.
38. *Ibid.*, p. 71.
39. *Ibid.*, p. 67.
40. *Ibid.*, p. 70.
41. *Ibid.*
42. *Ibid.*, p. 71.
43. *Ibid.*, p. 72.

8 / The Caroline Islands

1. *United Nations Trusteeship Council, 27th Session, 1 June–19 July 1961, T/SR.
1136–1176* (New York: 1961), p. 63.
2. "U.S. is Offering Concessions to the Micronesians' Demands for Home Rule,"
The New York Times, 24 December 1971, p. 6:1.
3. David S. Boyer, "Micronesia: The Americanization of Eden," *The Journal of the
National Geographic Society*, May 1967, p. 702–744.
4. "Continental Wins Micronesia Pact," *The New York Times*, 10 November 1967,
p. 93:7.
5. U.S. Dept. of State Bulletin, LV No. 1420 (Washington: U.S. Gov't. Print. Off.,
1966), p. 387–401.
6. "President Asks Pacific Trust Study," *The New York Times*, 22 August 1967,
p. 16:4.
7. Robert Trumbull, "Micronesia's Ties to Japan Growing," *The New York Times*,
12 November 1967, p. 12:1.

9 / The Mariana Islands

1. Harold J. Wiens, *Pacific Island Bastions of the United States* (Princeton: Van
Nostrand, 1962), p. 12.
2. Paul Carano and Pedro C. Sanchez, *A Complete History of Guam* (Rutland, Va.:
Charles E. Tuttle, Co., 1964), p. 8.
3. E. J. Kahn, Jr., "Micronesia," *The New Yorker*, 11 June 1966, p. 46.

4. P. H. Clyde, *Japan's Pacific Mandate* (New York: Macmillan, 1935), p. 14.

5. R. W. Robson, *The Pacific Islands Year Book* (Sydney: Pacific Publications (Fiji) Ltd., 1950), 6th ed., p. 187; see also, Carano and Sanchez, p. 122–127.

6. "Taking of the Ladrones," *The New York Times*, 5 July 1898, p. 2:3. Note the erroneous use of the plural. Actually only one of the Ladrones was taken by the United States, namely Guam.

7. Tadao Yanaihara, *Pacific Islands Under Japanese Mandate* (London and New York: Oxford University Press, 1940), p. 20.

8. Douglas L. Oliver, *The Pacific Islands*, rev. ed. (Garden City, New York: Doubleday, 1961), p. 239, 355.

9. A. Whitney Griswold, *The Far Eastern Policy of the United States* (New Haven and London: Yale University Press, 1938), p. 331.

10. Harold H. and Margaret T. Sprout, *Toward a New Order of Sea Power* (Princeton: Princeton University Press, 1940), p. 85. Italics not in the original.

11. Yanaihara, p. 30–31.

12. R. W. Robson, *The Pacific Islands Year Book*, 1942, 4th ed. (Sydney: Pacific Publications Pty., Ltd., 1942), p. 95.

13. Oliver, p. 355–356.

14. Robson, 4th ed., 1942, p. 95.

15. U.S. Dept. of the Interior, Fish and Wildlife Service, Fishery Leaflet #297, *The Japanese Tuna Fisheries* (April 1948), p. 17; as quoted in *Economic Development Plan for Micronesia* (Washington: Robert Nathan Associates, Inc., 1966), Part II, p. 274.

16. Price, p. 56.

17. Oliver, p. 355–356.

18. Masatake Okumiya, "For Sugar Boats or Submarines," *United States Naval Institute Proceedings*, August 1968, p. 66–73. See also, Thomas Wilds, "How Japan Fortified the Mandated Islands," *United States Naval Institute Proceedings*, April 1955, p. 400–407; and, O. R. Lodge, *The Recapture of Guam* (Washington: U.S. Govt. Print. Off., 1953), p. 167.

19. Carl W. Hoffman, *Saipan: The Beginning of the End* (Washington: U.S. Govt. Print. Off., 1950), p. 101.

20. *Ibid.*, p. 260.

21. Dorothy E. Richard, *United States Naval Administration of the Trust Territory of the Pacific Islands* (Washington: U.S. Govt. Print. Off., 1963), v. III.

22. R. Emerson, et. al., *America's Pacific Dependencies* (New York: American Institute of Pacific Relations, 1949), p. 8, as quoted in Richard, v. III, p. 80.

23. See for example a defense of the Navy's position in a letter from Secretary of the Navy James V. Forrestal, *The New York Times*, 24 September 1946, p. 28:6.

24. "Text of Trusteeship Proposal," *The New York Times*, 7 November 1946, p. 242.

25. Raymond Dennett and Robert K. Turner, eds., *Documents on American Foreign Relations* (Boston: World Peace Foundation, 1947), v. IX, p. 390.

26. *Ibid.*, p. 395.

27. "Navy to Control Saipan," *The New York Times*, 2 December 1952, p. 13:1.

28. U.S. Dept. of State, *Trust Territory of the Pacific Islands, 13th Annual Report*, 1960 (Washington: U.S. Govt. Print. Off., 1961), p. 8–9.

29. Whitney T. Perkins, *Denial of Empire: The United States and Its Dependencies* (Leyden, The Netherlands: Sythoff, 1962), p. 324.

30. Judy Tudor, ed., *Pacific Islands Year Book and Who's Who* (Sydney: Pacific Publications Pty., Ltd., 1963), 9th ed., p. 225.

31. Robert Trumbull, *Paradise in Trust: A Report on Americans in Micronesia, 1946–1958* (New York: William S. Sloane Associates, 1959), p. 15.

32. John Wesley Coulter, *The Pacific Dependencies of the United States* (New York: Macmillan, 1957), p. 171.

33. From 1953 until 1962 the Mariana Islands north of Rota were known as the "Saipan District."

34. Kahn, p. 62.

35. High Commissioner, *Trust Territory of the Pacific Islands—1967 Annual Report to the Secretary of the Interior* (Washington: U.S. Govt. Print. Off., 1967), p. 6–7.

36. M. W. Goding, *This is the Trust Territory of the Pacific Islands* (Saipan: High Commissioner, Trust Territory of the Pacific Islands, 1964), p. 1.

37. "Pacific Isles Under U.S.—They're in Bad Shape," *U.S. News and World Report*, 21 November 1966, p. 84.

38. U.S. Dept. of State, *Trust Territory of the Pacific Islands, 20th Annual Report, 1967* (Washington: U.S. Govt. Print. Off., 1968), p. 229. This will hereafter be referred to in the text and footnotes as "1967 Annual Report."

39. *Ibid.*, p. 233.

40. *Economic Development Plan for the Trust Territory of the Pacific Islands* (Washington: Robert R. Nathan Associates, Inc., 1966), p. 296–297. Hereafter referred to as the *Nathan Plan.*

41. Daniel J. Morgiewicz, "Micronesia *Especial* Trust," *United States Naval Institute Proceedings*, October 1968, p. 73.

42. "Johnson Asks Pacific Trust Study," *The New York Times*, 22 August 1967, p. 16:4.

·43. This was during the period of naval administration in the Northern Marianas. Out of a total of 2,847 registered voters, 2,517 voted to become citizens of the United States, either through unification with Guam or as a separate territory, and only 27 indicated a preference for the *status quo.*

44. Thomas R. Adam, *Western Interests in the Pacific Realm* (New York: Random House, 1967), p. 179.

45. Robert Trumbull, "Tie to U.S. Favored in Pacific Islands," *The New York Times*, 5 November 1967, p. 11:1.

46. "Report of the United Nations Visiting Mission to the Trust Territory of the Pacific Islands," 1964, p. 159, as quoted in Adam, p. 179.

47. Carano and Sanchez, p. 269.

48. Wiens, p. 119.

49. "New Defense Line in Pacific," *U.S. News and World Report*, 7 August 1967, p. 52.

50. "New Defense Line in Pacific," . . . p. 52.

51. *Ibid.*

52. Dennet and Turner, eds., v. IX, p. 395.

53. Hanson W. Baldwin, "After Vietnam—What Military Strategy in the Far East?", *The New York Times*, 9 June 1968, Section VI, p. 36.

54. *Ibid.* Italics not in the original.

55. "What U.S. is Giving Back to Japan," *U.S. News & World Report*, 27 November 1967, p. 54.

56. U.S. Congress, *Congressional Record—House*, 26 March 1968 (Washington: U.S. Govt. Print. Off., 1968), p. H2250. Hereafter referred to as Congressional Record, 26 March 1968.

57. Letter from Representative Patsy T. Mink, Congress of the United States, dated 11 February 1969 to the author.

58. *Ibid.*

59. Thomas R. Adam, "Our Neglected Pacific Neighbors," *The New York Times*, 4 February 1968, Section IV, p. 13:2. Dr. Adam is Professor of Political Science, New York University.

60. David S. Boyer, "Micronesia: The Americanization of Eden," *National Geographic Magazine*, May 1967, p. 724. See also *Nathan Plan.*

61. "Remembering an Adopted Cousin," *Time*, 23 May 1969, p. 28.

10 / The Marshall Islands

1. John Wesley Coulter, *The Pacific Dependencies of the United States* (New York: Macmillan, 1957), p. 294.

2. James A. Sugar, "Starfish threaten Pacific Reefs," *National Geographic*, March 1970, p. 340–352.

3. John Wesley Coulter, *The Pacific Dependencies of the United States*, (New York: Macmillan, 1957), p. 296–298.

4. E. J. Kahn, Jr., *A Reporter in Micronesia* (New York: Norton, 1966), p. 266.

5. John Wesley Coulter, p. 312–314.

6. *Ibid.*, p. 76.

7. John Wesley Coulter, p. 303.

8. *Ibid.*, p. 305.

9. *Ibid.*, p. 82.

10. *Ibid.*, p. 85.

11. *Ibid.*, p. 16.

Bibliography

Captain Dwight A. Lane, USN

BOOKS

Abend, Hallett. *Ramparts of the Pacific*. Garden City, N. Y.: Doubleday, Doran, 1942.

Adam, Thomas R. *Western Interests in the Pacific Realm*. New York: Random House, 1967.

Beaglehole, John C. *The Exploration of the Pacific*. London: A&C Black, 1934, 2nd. ed., 1947.

Belshaw, Cyril S. *Island Administration in the South West Pacific*. London: Royal Institute of International Affairs, 1950.

Benians, Ernest A., "The Western Pacific, 1788–1885," *Cambridge History of the British Empire*. Cambridge: Cambridge University Press, 1933.

Bentwich, Norman. *The Mandates System*. London: Longmans, 1930.

Borg, Dorothy. *The United States and the Far Eastern Crisis of 1933–1938*. Cambridge: Harvard University Press, 1964.

Brookes, Jean Ingram. *International Rivalry in the Pacific Islands, 1800–1875*. Berkeley: University of California Press, 1941.

Byrnes, James F. *Speaking Frankly*. New York: Harper, 1947.

Cammack, Floyd M. and Saito, Shiro. *Pacific Island Bibliography*. New York: Scarecrow Press, 1962.

Carano, Paul and Sanchez, Pedro C. *A Complete History of Guam*. Rutland, Va., Charles E. Tuttle, 1964.

Chowdhuri, Ramendra Nath. *International Mandates and Trusteeship Systems: A Comparative Study*. The Hague: Nijhoff, 1955.

Claude, Inis L., Jr. *Swords into Plowshares*. New York: Random House, 1959.

Clyde, Paul H. *Japan's Pacific Mandate*. New York: Macmillan, 1935.

Conover, Helen F., comp. *Islands of the Pacific: A Selected List of References*. Washington, D.C.: Library of Congress, 1943.

Current, Richard K. *Secretary Stimson: A Study in Statecraft*. New Brunswick, N.J., Rutgers University Press, 1954.

Davidson, James W. *The Study of Pacific History*. Canberra: 1955.

Doeker, Gunther. *The Treaty-Making Power in the Commonwealth of Australia*. The Hague: Martinus Nijhoff, 1966.

Emerson, Rupert, *America's Pacific Dependencies*. New York: American Institute of Pacific Relations, 1949.

————. *Self Determination Revisited in the Era of Decolonization*. Cambridge: Center for International Affairs, Harvard University, 1964.

Essai, Brian. *Papua and New Guinea*. Melbourne: Oxford University Press, 1961.

Fletcher, C. Brunsdon. *The Problem of the Pacific*. New York: Holt, 1919.

Friis, Herman R., ed. *The Pacific Basin: A History of Its Geographical Exploration*. American Geographical Society Special Publication No. 38. American Geographical Society, 1967.

Gelfand, Lawrence E. *The Inquiry: American Preparations for Peace, 1917–1919*. New Haven: Yale University Press, 1963.

Goding, M. W. *This is the Trust Territory of the Pacific Islands*. Saipan: High Commissioner, Trust Territory of the Pacific Islands, 1964.

Goodrich, Leland M. *The United Nations*. New York: Crowell, 1959.

Gordon, Bernard K. *New Zealand Becomes a Pacific Power*. Chicago: University of Chicago Press, 1960.

Grattan, C. Hartley. *The Southwest Pacific Since 1900*. Ann Arbor, Michigan: University of Michigan Press, 1963.

————. *The Southwest Pacific to 1900*. Ann Arbor, Michigan: University of Michigan Press, 1963.

Gray, John Alexander Clinton, *Amerika Samoa: a History of American Samoa and its United States Naval Administration.* Annapolis: U.S. Naval Institute, 1960.

Greenwood, Gordon. *Early American-Australian Relations: from the Arrival of the Spaniards in America to the Close of 1830.* Melbourne: Melbourne University Press, 1944.

Grew, Joseph C. *Ten Years in Japan.* New York: Simon and Schuster, 1944.

Griswold, A. Whitney. *The Far Eastern Policy of the United States.* New Haven: Yale University Press, 1938.

Hall, Hessel Duncan. *Mandates, Dependencies and Trusteeship.* Washington: Carnegie Endowment for International Peace, 1948.

Henderson, George Cockburn. *The Discoverers of the Fiji Islands.* London: John Murray, 1933.

Hoffman, Carl W. *Saipan: The Beginning of the End.* Washington: Historical Division, U.S. Marine Corps, 1950.

Hull, Cordell. *The Memoirs of Cordell Hull.* New York: Macmillan, 1948.

Kahn, E. J., Jr. *A Reporter in Micronesia.* New York: Norton, 1966

Kay, David A., ed. *The United Nations Political System.* New York: Wiley, 1967.

Keesing, Felix M. *Modern Samoa.* London: George Allen and Unwin, 1934.

————. *The South Seas in the Modern World.* New York: John Day, 1941.

Kimberley, Lewis A. "Samoa and the Hurricane of March 1889," *Papers of the Military Historical Society of Massachusetts.* Boston: Griffith-Stillings Press, 1902.

Larkin, T. C., ed. *New Zealand External Relations.* Wellington, New Zealand, Institute of Public Administration, London: Oxford University Press, 1962.

Lee, Marc J. *The United Nations and World Realities.* Oxford: Pergamon Press, 1962.

Leeson, Ida. *A Bibliography of Bibliographies of the South Pacific.* Oxford: Oxford University Press, 1954.

Livezey, William E. *Mahan on Sea Power*. Norman: University of Oklahoma Press, 1947.

Lloyd George, David. *Memoirs of the Peace Conference*. New Haven: Yale University Press, 1939.

Louis, Wm. Roger. *Great Britain and Germany's Lost Colonies*. Oxford: Clarendon Press, 1967.

Millis, Walter, ed. *The Forrestal Diaries*. New York: Viking, 1951.

McDonald, Alexander Hugh, ed. *Trusteeship in the Pacific*. Sydney: Angus and Robertson, 1949.

Morison, Samuel E. *Strategy and Compromise*. Boston: Little, Brown, 1958.

Morrell, W. P. *Britain in the Pacific Islands*. Oxford: Clarendon Press, 1960.

Murray, James N. *The United Nations Trusteeship System*. Urbana: University of Illinois Press, 1957.

Nathan, Robert R. *Economic Development Plan for Micronesia*. Washington: Robert Nathan Associates, 1967.

Oliver, Douglas L. *The Pacific Islands*. Cambridge: Harvard University Press, 1958.

Padelford, Norman J. and Goodrich, Leland M. eds. *The United Nations in the Balance*. New York: Praeger, 1965.

Perkins, Whitney T. *Denial of Empire: The United States and Its Dependencies*. Leyden, The Netherlands: A. W. Sythoff, 1962.

Pomeroy, Earl S. *Pacific Outpost: American Strategy in Guam and Micronesia*. Stanford: Stanford University Press, 1951.

Price, Sir Archibald Grenfell. *The Western Invasions of the Pacific and its Continents: A Study of Moving Frontiers and Changing Landscapes*.

Price, Willard. *Japan's Islands of Mystery*. New York: Day, 1944.

Reese, Trevor R. *Australia in the Twentieth Century*. New York: Praeger, 1964.

Richards, Dorothy E. *United States Naval Administration of the Trust Territories of the Pacific Islands*. Washington: U.S. Govt. Print. Off., 1963. 3v.

Robson, Robert W. *The Pacific Islands Handbook 1944.* New York: Macmillan, 1945.

Ross, Angus. *New Zealand Aspirations in the Pacific in the Nineteenth Century.* Oxford: Clarendon Press, 1964.

Russell, Ruth B. *A History of the United Nations Charter: the Role of the United States, 1940–45.* Washington: Brookings Institution, 1958.

Sady, Emil J. *The United Nations and Dependent Peoples.* Washington: Brookings Institution, 1956.

Scholefield, Guy H. *The Pacific: Its Past and Future.* London: Murray, 1919.

Sharp, Andrew. *The Discovery of the Pacific Islands.* Oxford: Clarendon Press, 1960.

Smith, Holland M. and Finch, Percy. *Coral and Brass.* New York: Scribners, 1949.

Sprout, Harold H. and Margaret I. *Toward a New Order of Sea Power.* Princeton, N.J.: Princeton University Press, 1940, 2nd ed.

Stanner, William E. H. *The South Seas in Transition: A Study of Post-War Rehabilitation and Reconstruction in Three British Pacific Dependencies.* Sydney: Australasian Publishing Co., 1953.

Starke, J. G. *The Anzus Treaty Alliance.* Melbourne: Melbourne University Press, 1965.

Taylor, Clyde R. H. *A Pacific Bibliography.* Oxford: Clarendon Press, 1965. 2nd ed.

Thomson, Robert P. *A National History of Australia, New Zealand and the Pacific Islands.* London: George Routledge and Sons, 1919.

Thullen, George. *Problems of the Trusteeship System.* Geneva: Librairie Droz, 1964.

Toussaint, Charmian Edwards. *The Trusteeship System of the United Nations.* London: Stevens, 1956.

Trumbull, Robert. *Paradise in Trust: A Report on Americans in Micronesia, 1946–1958.* New York: Sloane Associates, 1959.

Van Maanen-Helmer, Elizabeth. *The Mandates System in Relation to Africa and the Pacific Islands.* London: P. S. King, 1929.

Ward, John M. *British Policy in the South Pacific, 1786–1893: a Study in British policy towards the South Pacific Islands prior to the establishment of governments by the great powers.* Sydney: Australasian Pub. Co., 1948.

Watt, Alan S. *The Evolution of Australian Foreign Policy, 1938–1965.* London, Cambridge University Press, 1967.

West, F. J. *Political Advancement in the South Pacific: A Comparative Study of Colonial Practice in Fiji, Tahiti, and American Samoa.* Melbourne: Oxford University Press, 1961.

White, Freda. *Mandates.* London: Jonathan Cape, 1926.

Wiens, Harold J. *Pacific Island Bastions of the United States.* Princeton: Van Nostrand, 1962.

Wright, Quincy. *Mandates Under the League of Nations.* Chicago: University of Chicago Press, 1930.

Yanaihara, Tadao. *Pacific Islands Under Japanese Mandate.* London: Oxford University Press, 1940.

Zacharias, Captain Ellis M., U.S.N. *Secret Missions: The Story of an Intelligence Officer.* New York: Putnam, 1946.

ARTICLES

"Australia: Geographical Basis of Foreign Policy." *The Round Table,* March 1965, pp. 177–186.

"Australia: Our Mandate in New Guinea." *The Round Table,* September 1964, pp. 402–06.

Boyer, David S. "Micronesia: The Americanization of Eden." *The Journal of the National Geographic Society,* May 1967.

Burns, Richard Dean, "Inspection of the Mandates, 1919–1941." *Pacific Historical Review,* November 1968, pp. 445–62.

Corbett, D. C. "Problems of Australian Foreign Policy," *The Australian Journal of Politics and History,* May 1961, pp. 1–14.

Davidson, James W. "The Transition to Independence: the Example of Western Samoa." *The Australian Journal of Politics and History,* May 1961, pp. 15–40.

Gilchrist, Huntington. "The Japanese Islands: Annexation or Trusteeship?", *Foreign Affairs*, July 1944, pp. 635–42.

Haas, Ernst B. "The Reconciliation of Conflicting Colonial Policy Aims: Acceptance of the League of Nations Mandate System." *International Organization*, November 1952, pp. 521–36.

Hudson, W. J. "Australia's Experience as a Mandatory Power." *Australian Outlook*, April 1965, pp. 35–46.

Kay, David A. "The Politics of Decolonization: the New Nations and the United Nations Political Process." *International Organization*, Fall 1967, pp. 786–811.

Kerr, J. R. "Higher Education in New Guinea." *Australian Outlook*, December 1964, pp. 266–77.

————. "The Political Future of New Guinea." *Australian Outlook*, September 1959, pp. 181–92.

Legge, J. D. "Problems of Australian Foreign Policy." *The Australian Journal of Politics and History*, November 1960, pp. 139–52.

"The Literature of the Pacific Islands," *The Australian Outlook*, March 1947, pp. 63–79.

Mackee, J. A. C. "Inflation and Confrontation in Indonesia." *Australian Outlook*, December 1964, pp. 278–98.

Mead, Margaret. "The Rights of Primitive Peoples." *Foreign Affairs*, January 1967, pp. 304–18.

Morgiewicz, Cdr. Daniel J., USN, "Micronesia: Especial Trust." *United States Naval Institute Proceedings*, October 1968, pp. 68–79.

Okumiya, Lieutenant General Masatake. "For Sugar Boats or Submarines?" *United States Naval Institute Proceedings*, August 1968, pp. 66–73.

Pomeroy, Earl S. "American Policy Respecting the Marshalls, Carolines, and Marianas 1898–1941." *Pacific Historical Review*, February 1948.

Shand, R. T. "Some Obstacles to the Economic Development of Papua-New Guinea. *Australian Outlook*, December 1963, pp. 306–16.

Singh, L. P. "The Goal of Trusteeship-Self-Government or Independence." *Australian Outlook*, December 1961, pp. 295–306.

Van der Veur, Paul W. "The Political Future of Papua-New Guinea." *Australian Outlook*, August 1966, pp. 200–03.

———. "New Guinea Annexations and the Origin of the Irian Boundary." *Australian Outlook*, December 1964, pp. 313–39.

"Special Committee of Twenty-Four." *U.N. Monthly Chronicle*, March 1967, pp. 18–30.

"Territories Not Considered Separately." *U.N. Monthly Chronicle*, January 1968, pp. 80–83.

West, F. J. "The New Guinea Question: An Australian View." *Foreign Affairs*, April 1961, pp. 504–511.

Wilds, Thomas. "How Japan Fortified the Mandated Islands." *The United States Naval Institute Proceedings*, April 1955, pp. 401–07.

Windass, G. S. "Power Politics and Ideals: the Principle of Self-Determination." *International Relations*, October 1966, pp. 177–86.

Biographical Sketches

PROFESSOR WM. ROGER LOUIS received a Bachelor of Arts from the University of Oklahoma, a Master of Arts from Harvard University, and Doctor of Philosophy from Oxford University. He is the author of *Ruanda-Urundi, Germany's Lost Colonies*, and, with Professor Jean Stengers of the University of Brussels, *E. D. Morel's History of the Congo Reform Association*. In 1971 the Oxford University Press published his most recent major work, *British Strategy in the Far East, 1919–1939*. Professor Louis is also the co-editor with Dean Prosser Gifford of Amherst College of two Yale symposia, *Britain and Germany in Africa* and *France and Britain in Africa*. Formerly an associate professor at Yale University, he is now Professor of History at the University of Texas.

COMMANDER DAVID GLENN WILSON, U.S. Navy, holds a Bachelor of Science in Mechanical Engineering from Tulane University, a Bachelor of Science in Electrical Engineering from the Naval Postgraduate School and a Master of Science in International Affairs from George Washington University. He received an NROTC commission in 1954 and earned his wings as a fighter pilot the following summer. After a tour as a flight instructor, he underwent helicopter training and was assigned to Helicopter Anti-Submarine Squadron Eleven. He then served with Patrol Squadron Fourty-Four until he went to the Naval Postgraduate School. Upon graduation he was ordered to the Bureau of Naval Weapons, Washington, D.C., as the project officer of the Helicopter Attack System. This tour was followed by two years as Operations Officer of Patrol Squadron Twenty-Six in Brunswick, Maine, and ten months at the Naval War College, Newport, Rhode Island. He is presently assigned as the Executive Officer, Fleet Air Reconnaissance Squadron Four, Patuxent River, Maryland.

CAPTAIN WILLIAM O. MILLER, Judge Advocate General Corps, U.S. Navy, graduated from the University of South Carolina, and holds a Bachelor of Laws from Atlanta Law School, a Master of Law and a Master of Science in International Affairs from George Washington University. He is a graduate of the Naval War College, School of Naval Warfare. His Navy Legal Officer assignments include duty with the Office of the Judge Advocate General as Appellate Counsel and Executive Assistant in the International Law Division as the Assistant Legal Officer, Hq. Commander U.S. Naval Forces Philippines; Assistant Legal Officer, Hq. 14th Naval District; and Assistant Legal Officer, U.S. Fleet. He has served as Legal Advisor to the Director of the Joint Staff, Office of the Joint Chiefs of Staff; and as Deputy Assistant Judge Advocate General for International Law. He is currently serving as Deputy Assistant Judge Advocate General for Administrative Law.

COLONEL GEORGE H. DODENHOFF, U.S.M.C., has flown combat missions against the Japanese on Okinawa, was a pilot in the Korean conflict and has headed Marine air intelligence in Vietnam. The Colonel's varied assignments included a tour as an exchange officer to the U.S. Air Force. In 1954–55 he commanded a fighter squadron of the USAF in France. In 1962 he was involved in the Cuban missile crisis as chief of staff for Landing Force Aviation and, two years later, directed airlift support operations for the embattled government forces in the Congo. Colonel Dodenhoff was commanding officer of the Marine Air Reserve Training Detachment/Marine Aircraft Group 43 at Willow Grove, Pa., from 1968–70, and is now serving at Headquarters Marine Corps, Washington, D.C.

COMMANDER WILLIAM D. MUNSEY, U.S. Navy, entered Navy flight training at Pensacola, Florida in February 1955. He was designated a naval aviator in September 1956, and his first duty station was with Air Anti-Submarine Squadron 38 in San Diego, California. Following several operational tours to the western Pacific, Commander Munsey was assigned to Washington, D.C. in 1961 for duty in the Officer Promotions Branch of the Bureau of Naval Personnel. He returned to operational flying in September 1964, this time in the Atlantic and Mediterranean with Air Anti-Submarine Squadron 36. This assignment was followed by a tour on the staff of Commander in Chief, U.S. Naval Forces Europe, based in London. He attended the Naval War College in 1968–69, after which he was Aircraft Handling Officer aboard USS *Hornet*, the astronaut recovery ship for Apollo 11 and 12. Commander Munsey is currently serving on the staff of Commander in Chief Pacific in Honolulu, Hawaii.

CAPTAIN JOHN L. BUTTS is a 1951 graduate of the United States Naval Academy and holds a master's degree in International Affairs from The George Washington University. He has served in USS *McKean*, USS *Sterlet*, USS *Bashaw* and USS *Bream*. From 1957 to 1960 he was assistant to the Naval Aide to President Eisenhower and he has completed two other tours in Washington, both with the Office of Naval Intelligence. His overseas assignments have included a brief period of duty in Indonesia, a tour in the Philippines and a recently completed assignment as a staff officer at Supreme Headquarters Allied Powers Europe in Belgium. He is currently assigned to the Defense Intelligence Agency in Washington.

CAPTAIN DWIGHT LANE, U.S. Navy, a 1946 graduate of the U.S. Naval Academy, has had duties in intelligence, photographic interpretation, and anti-submarine warfare. In the Korean War he served in the USS *Essex*. Later he commanded Patrol Squadron Two, operating from the Aleutians to Saigon. During the Vietnam War he was executive officer of the USS *Princeton*. He has served in the Office of the Chief of Naval Operations, the Naval Air Systems Command, and in Germany. Captain Lane is a 1970 graduate of the Naval War College and he received a Master of Science in International Affairs from George Washington University in 1970. He is now the first U.S. Naval Attaché to the Independent State of Western Samoa as well as Naval Attaché to New Zealand.

COLONEL LAWRENCE E. ADAMS, U.S. Army is currently the Commanding Officer of the 160 5h Signal Group in Vietnam. His previous assignments have included telecommunications advisor to the National Military Command System, Organization of the Joint Chiefs of Staff, Washington, D.C.; Commanding Officer, Pentagon Telecommunications Facilities, U.S. Army Strategic Communications Command; J–6 Staff Officer, Headquarters Military Assistance Command, Vietnam; Chief, International Circuit Ordering Agency, Paris, France; Radio Officer, 8th Army, Korea. He is a graduate of the Army Command and General Staff College, the Armed Forces Staff College, and the Naval War College where he was selected as a distinguished graduate in 1968. He holds a Master of Science in International Affairs from George Washington University.

COLONEL CLYDE W. HUNTER enlisted in the Marine Corps following the attack on Pearl Harbor and saw action in the Marshalls and at Saipan, Tinian, and Iwo Jima. He received a field promotion from platoon sergeant to second lieutenant before World War II ended. He commanded a tank company for a year in the Korean War and an infantry regiment in Vietnam, followed by a tour as Assistant Chief of Staff, G–3, Fleet Marine Force, Seventh Fleet. He has served as operations officer at battalion, regiment, and division levels, as plans officer at Headquarters Marine Corps and Headquarters Fleet Marine Force, Pacific, and as Chief of Staff, Force Troops, Fleet Marine Force, Pacific. Currently, he is Assistant Commander, Force Troops and Marine Corps Base, Twentynine Palms, California. Colonel Hunter has completed the Army Advanced Armored Course and the Marine Corps Amphibious Warfare Course and the Naval Warfare Course at Naval War College. He has a Bachelor of Science from the University of Nebraska at Omaha and a Master of Science in International Affairs from George Washington University.

COLONEL PAUL B. HAIGWOOD holds a Bachelor of Science in Business Administration from the University of North Carolina, and a Master of Arts in Personnel Management and Master of International Affairs from the George Washington University. During World War II he served as a platoon commander in Hawaii, Okinawa, Japan, and Guam, and subsequently as company commander in Korea. After various assignments at Headquarters, U.S. Marine Corps, Colonel Haigwood attended the Thai Language School and was assigned as Senior Advisor, Royal Thai Marine Corps. He then served in Vietnam. Following service in Vietnam, Colonel Haigwood was a Battalion

Commander with the Sixth Marine Regiment. Upon graduation from the Naval War College in 1969, Colonel Haigwood was selected as a Distinguished Graduate of the School of Naval Warfare. He is presently Chief of Staff, Second Marine Division.

COMMANDER FREDERIC L. NYSTROM, U.S. Navy, entered the Naval Reserve Officers Training Corps at the University of Michigan in 1949 and received a Bachelor of Arts in Political Science in 1953 from the University of Minnesota. He served in Patrol Squadron One and Patrol Squadron Six, as a flight instructor in the Naval Air Basic Training Command, and as Administrative Officer of Utility Wing Pacific. He has attended the Defense Intelligence School in Washington, D.C. and served as the Special Security Officer and Special Activities Officer, Staff of the Commander in Chief Pacific. He attended the Naval War College, and holds a master's degree in International Affairs. He was Executive Officer of Heavy Attack Squadron Twenty-one, and is now Aviation Officer on the staff of the Amphibious Warfare Board.

COMMANDER JOHN R. LINCOLN, U.S. Navy, is a graduate of the Southeast Missouri State College and of the Meteorological Curriculum, U.S. Naval Postgraduate School, Monterey, California. He holds a master's degree from George Washington University and is a 1969 graduate of the Naval War College, School of Naval Command and Staff. His assignments in the U.S. Navy include: Forecaster, U.S. Fleet Weather Central, Port Lyautey, Morocco; Hurricane Forecaster and Assistant Research Officer, Fleet Hurricane Forecast Facility, Miami, Florida; Assistant Meteorological Officer and Flight Meteorologist for the Navy's Hurricane Hunter Squadron; Assistant Director, Joint Typhoon Warning Center, Guam, Mariana Islands, and Navy Plans and

Programs Officer, Headquarters, Naval Weather Service Command, Washington, D.C. In August 1969, Commander Lincoln assumed command of the U.S. Fleet Weather Facility, Yokosuka, Japan. He has had additional duty as the

Staff Meteorologist for Commander U.S. Naval Forces, Japan. Since January 1971 his assignment has been in USS *America* as the meteorological officer with additional duty as the Staff Meteorologist for the embarked staff. Commander Lincoln is currently serving in the Headquarters, Naval Weather Service Command, Washington Navy Yard.

CAPTAIN ROBERT W. THOMPSON, Supply Corps, U.S. Navy, was graduated from the U.S. Naval Academy in 1946. He has attended the Navy Management Postgraduate School, Monterey, California, and the School of Naval Warfare, U.S. Naval War College; he obtained a master's degree in International Affairs from the George Washington University. He has been assigned to the USS *Noa*, USS *Warrington*, USS *Frybarger*, USS *Hunley*, and to Staff ComDesFlot Six. His shore duties include the Naval Air Station, Brunswick, Maine; Naval Supply Center, Pearl Harbor; Staff Inspector General, Supply Corps; Naval Shipyard, Charleston, South Carolina; and the Strategic Systems Projects Office. He has served as Supply and Fiscal Officer, Naval Support Activity, Saigon, as Deputy Director, Naval Audit Service, and as Deputy Auditor General of the Navy. In 1971 Captain Thompson became Acting Director, Naval Audit Service, with additional duty as Acting Auditor General of the Navy.

Index